"As someone who has read and tau
fiction continually for the past half
riveted by Angela Alaimo O'Donne
readable biography of one of the twentieth century's most deeply
fascinating writers. What O'Donnell has managed to do here is
to get at the heart of the mystery of O'Connor's novels, short
stories, essays, and letters and to reveal the by turns dark and
luminous Catholic faith that sustained and transformed her work
throughout her too-brief life. The truth is I could not put
O'Donnell's book down until I had read straight through it from
beginning to end. It's all here—the scholarship, the critical
insights, a Catholic writer's trenchant understanding of another
Catholic writer to remind us that the spirit of Merton, Dorothy
Day, Walker Percy, and O'Connor herself is alive and well today."

—Paul Mariani
Boston College

"Angela Alaimo O'Donnell has written a graceful, compelling
biography of Flannery O'Connor whose fiction, she rightfully
insists, constituted 'the inestimable contribution [she] has made
to American Catholic literature, thought, and culture.' A devout
Catholic, O'Connor wrote with the same fervor about her faith
than she did her craft. Seamlessly moving from the life events in
O'Connor's pilgrimage—the places she wrote, the friends she
made, the sufferings she endured—into the characters, settings,
and symbols of her stories, O'Donnell brings readers into that
enlightened nexus where O'Connor's Catholicism explains and
extolls her art. O'Donnell's biography is a must read for anyone
who wants to understand how and why O'Connor's fiction
with its violence, suffering, and mystery emerges from her
Roman Catholic faith and practice."

—Philip C. Kolin
University of Southern Mississippi
Editor, *The Southern Quarterly*

Flannery O'Connor

Fiction Fired by Faith

Angela Alaimo O'Donnell

LITURGICAL PRESS
Collegeville, Minnesota

www.litpress.org

1   2   3   4   5   6   7   8   9

Library of Congress Control Number: 2014950491

ISBN 978-0-8146-3701-2   978-0-8146-3726-5 (ebook)

For Brennan

Contents

Abbreviations

Acknowledgments

It is a commonplace that biographers stand on the shoulders of those who have come before them, and this is certainly true of my experience in writing this brief biography of Flannery O'Connor. I have relied on documents produced by many people, beginning with O'Connor, herself, followed by Sally Fitzgerald, who did the foundational work of editing O'Connor's letters and essays and in creating the detailed chronology of her life published in *The Collected Works*. Publication of the letters, in particular, has made it possible for O'Connor to narrate her own story, in a sense, and for us to hear it told in her own voice.

This book owes a great debt to two biographies that have provided faithful and compelling accounts of O'Connor's life—Paul Elie's *The Life You Save May Be Your Own: An American Pilgrimage* and Brad Gooch's *Flannery: A Life of Flannery O'Connor*. These biographers have constructed narratives that enable readers to see the external circumstances of O'Connor's life as well as the internal workings provided in her letters, consulted archives containing writings only recently available, conducted interviews with O'Connor's friends and colleagues, and offered insightful commentary on the connections between her life and her work. To the reader eager to know more about O'Connor's life, I heartily recommend both books.

In addition, I owe a great debt to the many scholars who have written critical studies of O'Connor's work. These writers are too many to name, but I'm especially grateful for the work of Jill Peleaz Baumgaertner, Sr. Kathleen Feeley, SSND, and Richard Giannone. In my years of teaching, I have availed myself of their fine scholarship and their often brilliant analyses of O'Connor's fiction, and they have shaped my own understanding of her work.

On a more personal note, there are a number of people I would like to thank for their roles in making this book possible. First, I am grateful to the staff at Liturgical Press, especially Barry Hudock, for inviting me to write a biography of Flannery O'Connor for the "People of God" series. It has been a pleasure and privilege to devote so much time and energy to careful consideration of O'Connor's life and work.

I am grateful to my colleagues at Fordham University's Curran Center for American Catholic Studies, Christine Firer Hinze and Maria G. Terzulli, for their enthusiasm about this project and for their unflagging support of my work. I am blessed to work at such a rich and vibrant center and in partnership with such generous colleagues.

I am grateful for the support I received from the Collegeville Institute for Ecumenical & Cultural Research in the form of a writing residency in the Ecclesial Literature Project's "Apart, and yet a Part" workshop. Inspired by my colleagues in the program and by our writing coach, Michael McGregor, I wrote key portions of the manuscript during my time there and benefited from Michael's insightful critique and commentary.

Finally, I'd like to express my deepest gratitude to my family, especially to my husband, Brennan, for his love and long friendship and for his unfailing support and encouragement of my work. His fine critical eye and his ear for the rhythms of good prose have made this a better book. The fact that we "discovered" O'Connor together as undergraduates and spent many years reading her stories, talking about them, and teaching them to our own students has led us both to a constantly deepening appreciation of and affection for her work. In a sense, Flannery has been a member of our household for three decades. For these reasons and more, this book is dedicated to him.

Introduction

Flannery O'Connor is, perhaps, the most celebrated American Catholic writer of the twentieth century—and justly so. The author of thirty-two short stories, two novels, insightful essays on the craft of fiction, and hundreds of splendid, literary letters, O'Connor devoted herself to her vocation as artist and belongs to that unusual breed of writer who gains critical acclaim during her lifetime. That recognition is hard won for O'Connor, as the literary establishment is generally suspicious of writers who claim allegiance to a particular faith. On more than one occasion, readers of her work remarked on her Catholicism, and not in a complimentary way. In 1972, when her publisher Robert Giroux was preparing himself to receive the National Book Award O'Connor was posthumously awarded for her *Collected Stories,* an author startled him by inquiring whether he genuinely valued her work: "Do you really think Flannery O'Connor was a great writer? She's such a Roman Catholic!"[1] The implication is clear: being a practicing Catholic somehow disqualifies a writer from serious consideration, as if one's art is marred by belief in God or one's mind is compromised by adherence to the teachings of the church—or both.

Despite this deep cultural prejudice against Catholics—a prejudice that has flourished in America from its early Puritan beginnings—O'Connor managed to write fiction that was so arresting and original that perceptive readers could not help but recognize her genius. During her brief lifetime—cut sadly short by lupus, the disease she suffered with for thirteen years before her death at age thirty-nine—she won many awards for her fiction, including grants from the National Institute of Arts and Letters and the Ford Foundation, a fellowship from the *Kenyon Review*, and several O. Henry awards. As mentioned above, her posthumous collection, *The Complete Stories,* received the National Book Award in 1972. This extraordinary event marked a break with tradition—the award, usually given to a living writer, was granted to O'Connor's work by the judges to honor her lifetime achievement. Clearly, as both an American writer and as a Catholic writer, Flannery O'Connor has achieved a rare distinction: recognition of the value of her work by the literary establishment as well as by readers in search of a voice and vision that can articulate the challenges of enacting belief in a culture of unbelief.

Finding Flannery

It seems some account of my own relationship to Flannery O'Connor's work is in order—and I'm going to begin with a spoiler.

When I first encountered O'Connor's fiction as an undergraduate English major at a secular university, I didn't know she was Catholic. We read her signature story, "A Good Man Is Hard to Find," in a literature course, along with works by other celebrated authors, including Henry James, William Faulkner, and Vladamir Nabokov. A strange tale, depicting a road trip that goes horribly wrong when the family encounters a serial killer along the back roads of Georgia, O'Connor's story is both humorous and terrifying. The main character, a garrulous old grandmother regarded as a nuisance and a busybody by her family, is slightly ridiculous. She is the kind of woman who sneaks her cat into the car (hidden in her hippopotamus-shaped suitcase) because she is afraid he'll accidentally turn on the gas stove in her absence and asphyxiate himself, the kind of woman who wears a nice dress, gloves, and a fancy hat when she travels in case she should get into an accident so that anyone who might see her lying dead on the side of the road will know that she is a lady. At the end of the story, this absurd woman comes face-to-face with her own doom in the form of a bespectacled outlaw called "The Misfit" who is tortured by his inability to believe in God. Much to her grief and disbelief, the man has led her entire family into the woods and summarily executed each member. All of this is remarkable, to say the least—not the kind of story one reads every day. But what is most remarkable is the grandmother's response to the Misfit's near-tears expression of his spiritual agony. Amid her urgings that he must have faith in the God he doubts, she extends her hand in attempt to comfort him, referring to him as "one of my own babies," whereupon he promptly shoots her three times in the chest. The last we see of the grandmother, she is lying dead in a ditch, her legs crossed beneath her and her face turned up towards the blue Georgia sky. She is smiling.

As a nineteen-year-old reader, relatively unschooled in the ways of literary criticism, I had no idea what to make of such a story. Was I supposed to feel sorry for the grandmother and her family? (Truth be told, they were foolish and annoying enough to stretch any reader's patience.) Was

I was supposed to despise the Misfit? (He was a terrible man, but he was also agonized by his unbelief.) Was I supposed to laugh at the comic touches that coexist side-by-side with the tragic reality of a serial killing? (The fact that the grandmother's son, Bailey, wears a ridiculous yellow shirt with large blue parakeets on it as he disappears into the woods—and that his killer emerges from the woods wearing that same shirt—seemed grimly funny and horrible at the same time.) Was I supposed to think the grandmother deranged in her response to the Misfit's spiritual crisis? (She was, in fact, traumatized by the day's events.) Or was this a calculated, last-ditch effort to save herself? (The old woman could be cagey, selfish, and manipulative.) Finally, how was I supposed to make sense of these apparently senseless deaths?

O'Connor's story shocked us all, back then, and as a longtime professor of literature, I can attest that it still shocks students today. (Yes, even now, despite their exposure to many more images of brutality represented in film and on television than college-age students of my generation had ever seen.) I wanted to understand what this writer was up to, but my English professor at the time didn't provide very much help. We examined the story as one of many stories we read that semester, each of which contained unaccountable ambiguities. There were no satisfying answers to the questions we posed. Instead, we were to accept the strangeness and move on.

A few years later, when I encountered O'Connor's work again as a graduate student studying literature, I learned that she was Catholic. In addition, she was a Catholic born and raised in the (then) largely anti-Catholic South. Interestingly, I happened to be enrolled in a Southern university at the time and had witnessed, firsthand, how rare Catholics were in that part of the world. Having grown up in the Northeast in a region where the dominant religion was Catholicism, this sensation of not belonging was new to me. For the first time in my life, as a Catholic I was considered foreign and exotic. Suddenly, in my new environment, I was able to re-see Flannery O'Connor as a fellow Catholic-in-exile (though perhaps I was being a shade dramatic) and to re-see her stories, including "A Good Man Is Hard to Find," as the work of an unmistakably Catholic writer.

Viewed through the lens of O'Connor's faith, I came to understand the story in an entirely new light. In the simplest terms, what she had captured so powerfully and hauntingly in the conflict between the grandmother and the Misfit was the struggle between faith and doubt in the face of human suffering. The story was not an isolated tale of horror, but a universal moral drama, an externalized *psychomachia* representing the battle that goes on in every human soul. I recognized the grandmother's foolishness as garden variety human folly, the family's intolerance of her typical of intergenerational family dynamics, and the fate that befalls them all as the result of dumb, blind chance—events terrible, undeserved, yet somehow inevitable. This was a representation of the human condition, though expressed in the most vivid and local terms. It was also an expression of the human plight: Evil exists in the world, in this case in the form of the Misfit, and it is often performed by people who don't seem particularly evil. Far from being consummate devils, readily recognizable by horns and hoofs, they are ordinary, awkward, foolish human beings, often more like us than not. This shared capacity for good and for evil is precisely what the grandmother in the story recognizes, what causes an upwelling of compassion in her, and what compels her to reach out to the Misfit. Seen in the context of Catholic theology, I understood

the Grandmother's final actions not as a crazy woman's de-
lusional gesture, but as a sign of her conversion and transformation, the action of grace in her soul. The last gesture in
the life of this selfish woman is a self-forgetful expression of
love. Yes, it gets her killed—because the world O'Connor
depicts is, after all, the real world, and serial killers *are* killers.
But by her actions, her life is redeemed. Her death, therefore,
is not a tragedy—quite the contrary. (Hence the crossed legs
and the smile.) The depiction of her at the end of the story
indicates the peace of mind and heart she has found through
her Christlike action. Here, too, is a reminder of both the real
world and the ways in which it is a challenge to live one's
faith in that world: Christ was crucified for his unaccountable
gestures of love—why should his followers expect any different treatment? O'Connor, herself, confirms this understanding of the story. In a letter to her friend Elizabeth Hester
she writes: "It seems to me that all good stories are about
conversion, about a character's changing. . . . All my stories
are about the action of grace on a character who is not very
willing to support it, but most people think of these stories
as hard, hopeless, brutal. . . ."[2] Clearly, O'Connor sees hope
in the actions of her characters where others (mistakenly) see
despair.

Keeping Company with O'Connor

My discovery of the grandmother's conversion—and,
ultimately, her salvation—also marked a kind of conversion
in me. Recognition of O'Connor's Catholicism, and the fact
that her fiction was informed by her faith, encouraged me
to explore her work more fully and to realize the degree to
which her religious belief shaped her imagination. I would
go on to read the rest of O'Connor's stories, her novels, her

essays and lectures, and her many letters, during my time in graduate school. The letters, in particular, enabled me to trace O'Connor's journey from literary apprentice, unsure of her talents, to mature writer in full possession of the knowledge of her work's worth. They also enabled me to bear witness to O'Connor's deepening understanding of her faith. O'Connor's theological reading was broad as it was voracious, ranging from the writings of the church fathers and those of the saints to works by contemporary theologians such as Romano Guardini and Pierre Teilhard de Chardin. As she struggled with the disease that would eventually kill her, O'Connor retained her intellectual acuity and her unfailing sense of humor. The subject of her own imminent mortality was never very far from her mind, but rather than making her morbid, this knowledge made her receptive to reality, to the plain fact of death, and to the urgent necessity of preparing for what lies beyond this life. She eventually came to see her illness as yet another form of grace: "I have never been anywhere but sick. In a sense, sickness is a place, more instructive than a long trip to Europe, and it's always a place where there's no company; where nobody can follow. Sickness before death is a very appropriate thing and I think those who don't have it miss one of God's mercies."[3]

O'Connor's journey took her to places she did not wish to go, but the pilgrimage made her more fully human, more faithful, and more attentive to the life around her—the life that would be the substance of her stories.

Through this process of accompaniment, I gained a sense of intimacy with O'Connor. Her strange stories gradually opened up for me, though I confess I still found them puzzling and challenging. Her astonishing ability to present the world we think we know in unexpected guises continually surprised me, kept me guessing, and goaded me into reading more deeply and attentively in the hope of discovering the truths that lie at the core of her vision. There is always something dark, elusive, and mysterious about an O'Connor story—just as there is inevitable mystery at the center of the faith she professed—and it was that element of mystery that compelled me to return to her work again and again.

Fortunately for me, I have been able to devote a good portion of my life, as both a reader and a teacher, to attending to that mystery at the center of O'Connor's fiction. In my thirty years as a professor, I have taught her stories innumerable times, and with each fresh encounter, I find something new to admire in O'Connor's vision and her craft. In a sense, we have undertaken a common pilgrimage as we navigate the many intersections of art and faith. In addition, I am able to do this in partnership with my students, most of whom are reading O'Connor's work for the first time. Keenly aware of my own initial response to her fiction in my sophomore classroom so many years ago, I know how troubling they may find it. Perhaps that's why I feel particularly privileged to serve as their guide through the complexities of her stories. As a teacher in a Catholic Studies program at a Jesuit university, I am able to ground O'Connor's fiction in the fact of her faith—something my professors at a secular university were unwilling or unable to do—to discuss her stories in light of the theology of Catholicism, and to enable my students to experience the kind of conversion I did, recognizing the ways in which grace and redemption work in the lives of even the most (seemingly) undeserving of characters, as well as (seemingly) undeserving human beings.

As is evident, my fascination with O'Connor extends beyond her fiction. A deep interest in a writer's work inevitably leads to a deep interest in his or her life, and in the case of

O'Connor, it is impossible to study her life without reckoning with the primacy of her faith. Conversely, as my own discovery described above suggests, knowledge of the life of a writer enhances a reader's understanding of his or her work. This knowledge is particularly necessary for a writer like O'Connor, who is very deliberate in presenting her readers with situations that shock readers out of their complacency and challenge ordinary ways of thinking. This book is an attempt to provide for the reader a brief account of the life of Flannery O'Connor demonstrating some of the ways in which her fiction, like a finely wrought piece of pottery, is both shaped and fired by her faith. My hope is that readers who are new to her work, or readers who have encountered her work and found it peculiar or puzzling, will arrive at a fuller understanding of the stories themselves, but also a fuller sense of Flannery O'Connor as a human being. As a conversationalist and correspondent, she was brilliant, witty, hilarious, charming, stubborn, and eccentric. As an artist, she was ambitious for her work and yet humble before her art. As a Catholic, she believed passionately in her faith—was free of pieties and yet respectful of the church—and cultivated the connection between her twin vocations as an artist and as a devout believer. Given all of this, it is small wonder that we continue to value, half a century after her death, the inestimable contribution O'Connor has made to American Catholic literature, thought, and culture. In addition to telling her story, this brief study will attempt to assess the nature and scope of that contribution. I hope it might prove an invitation to the reader to follow O'Connor beyond these pages, to (re)read her marvelous work, and to keep company with her as she explores the nuances of her faith by means of her art.

CHAPTER ONE

The Road from Savannah
to Milledgeville (1925–45)

Memories of a Catholic Girlhood

"As for biographies, there won't be any biographies
of me because, for only one reason, lives spent between the house and the chicken yard do not make
exciting copy."[1]

—Letter to Betty Hester, 1958

Flannery O'Connor knew a good story when she read—
or wrote—one. Given this, it is ironic, perhaps, that she did
not see the drama and grandeur of her own. While it's true
that the details of O'Connor's life do not constitute tabloid
fare—there are no scandals, no torrid love affairs, no bouts
of madness, no amassing (or loss) of enormous wealth, no
rise to stardom, and no subsequent fall to obscurity—it is
the quiet ordinariness of her story that makes it remarkable.
The outline of her life is spare, elegant, and easily traceable.
Born and raised in the state of Georgia, Flannery lived there
until her college graduation. Afterwards, the world opened

up for her when she went to graduate school at the Iowa Writers' Workshop, where she encountered influential writers who would admire and help promote her work. As a result of these connections, O'Connor would move to New York City, the center of the writing and publishing world, and take up residence in Connecticut with friends who wished to provide her with space wherein her writing would flourish. Just as O'Connor seemed poised on the brink of success—having drafted her first novel and found a publisher at age twenty-five—the diagnosis of lupus sent her back to Georgia, back to the family farm she knew as a child, which bore the exotic name "Andalusia," and back to a state of childlike dependency as she would live with her mother who cared for her in her debilitating sickness until she died. It was during her thirteen-year sojourn at Andalusia that she wrote the words in the epigraph to this chapter. From her vantage point, her life was "as ordinary as a loaf of bread," to quote the words of one of her characters, O. E. Parker of "Parker's Back," a man who is sorely in need of recovering a sense of his own wonder. This statement is surely an expression of O'Connor's humility and perhaps a manifestation of her disappointment—but it is also, characteristically, a criticism of readers' expectations when it comes to biography (or fiction, for that matter). Readers want to be amused, excited, titillated, shocked, and surprised. She saw little in her own life that would evoke those emotions, so she had to content herself with obscurity—or so she thought.

In truth, O'Connor's earthly pilgrimage was brief and poignant. In some ways, this poignancy is inevitable when a talented person dies before she is able to fulfill her promise. But in O'Connor's case, we are moved by her life—by her death—and by the particulars of her journey because through her stories, essays, and, especially, her letters, we get to know her extraordinarily well. During the time when O'Connor was living in exile—walking from the house to the chicken yard and back—she was corresponding with friends and fellow writers, publishers, readers, and fans of her work. Reading these letters, we become eavesdroppers overhearing stories of every kind, ranging from her delight in the peafowl she raises to her pleasure at meeting a quirky couple at the doctor's office who reminds her of a pair of her own characters; from her steely disapproval of the suggestions made by an editor regarding a piece of her work to her enthusiastic admiration of her favorite writers; from profound theological insights she gains from her reading to the generous spiritual direction she provides for readers who write to her about matters of faith. We also bear witness to O'Connor's courage, gratitude, and irrepressible grace in the face of the disease that is gradually ravaging her body. By the time death arrives, the reader feels very much as if he or she has lost a friend and fellow-traveling companion along the pilgrimage of life. Contrary to O'Connor's assessment, hers is a story well worth reading and worth telling. As with any good story, it's best to begin at the beginning.

Arrival & Early Stirrings

Mary Flannery O'Connor was born on March 25, 1925, to Edward and Regina Cline O'Connor at St. Joseph's Hospital in the city of Savannah, Georgia. In choosing her first name, her devoutly-Catholic parents acknowledged the auspicious day of their daughter's birth, the Feast of the Annunciation. In choosing her middle name, they harkened back to the Cline family's august Southern past, preserving the memory of Civil War Captain John Flannery, who later became a wealthy banker and cotton broker, and his wife, Mary Ellen Flannery. Thus, from the beginning, O'Connor's dual identity as Catholic and Southerner was established. (O'Connor would later drop the name *Mary*, when she began writing in earnest, judging the name *Mary O'Connor* an insufficiently interesting or memorable pen name.)

O'Connor's family was thoroughly Irish Catholic on both sides, though their backgrounds and history were markedly different. Her maternal great-grandfather, Hugh Donnelly Treanor, had immigrated to America from County Tipperary in 1824 and settled in Milledgeville in central Georgia where he made his name and his fortune operating a water-powered gristmill on the Oconee River. O'Connor reports in one of her letters that the first Mass in Milledgeville was said in his hotel room, and future Masses would take place in his home where the priest would use the piano as an altar.[2] Regina Lucille Cline was born into a family that was large (she was one of sixteen children), prosperous (they lived in an antebellum mansion), and influential (her father was elected town mayor in 1889). In contrast, Flannery's father came from a more humble background. His grandfather, Patrick O'Connor, immigrated to Savannah in 1851 where he established a livery stable, and his father worked as a wholesale distributor. Though his father was successful enough as a businessman, Edward O'Connor was not a child of wealth or privilege. When he and Regina met at a family wedding, he was twenty-six-years old, living with his parents, and working as a salesman in his father's business. Regina, too, was twenty-six, and recently recovered from a love affair gone wrong. O'Connor was strikingly handsome, charming, and a decorated soldier, having been awarded a World War I Victory Medal. Within three months of their meeting, they were engaged and married soon afterwards at the Sacred Heart Church in Milledgeville. The couple then established themselves in the fashionable Irish Catholic enclave of Lafayette Square (with the financial assistance of Regina's relatives) in Savannah. The tensions inherent in such a "mixed" marriage would manifest themselves from time to time, but O'Connor's parents were affectionate towards one another and were equally smitten with their only child, though as she grew they would show their love in different ways—her father in undisguised and unconditional delight at his daughter's talents, and her mother in her devotion to the task of raising her daughter to be a proper Southern lady.

In "Memories of a Catholic Boyhood," the preface to his book about Catholicism in America, writer Garry Wills describes life for Catholic children during the pre-Vatican II era: "We grew up different." In his essay, Wills captures the experience of the Catholic raised in a largely Protestant culture—for Catholics, being different was a point of pride. In the Savannah of O'Connor's childhood, Irish Catholics were a considerable presence. Many Irish had arrived during the potato famines of the 1840s, many had demonstrated their loyalty to their home state and region by fighting in the Civil War (as did Captain Flannery), and some had gone on to hold leadership positions in local government. However, Catholics were still regarded with suspicion and treated with prejudice. Anti-Catholic laws were still on the books, and though Catholics did not have to endure the Jim Crow laws that strictly divided the city by race, there was an invisible, *de facto* line of separation that kept the Irish Catholics segregated. Lafayette Square, the "better" section of the Catholic ghetto where the O'Connors lived, was situated at the center of the Catholic life in Savannah. Within sight of the Cathedral of St. John the Baptist (and in audible range of the *Angelus* bells), forty yards from the Catholic grammar school she would attend, surrounded by like-minded observant Catholic neighbors, Flannery grew up "different," indeed, from the non-Catholic children of the city. Their daily lives governed by the liturgical calendar, Saints' Days and Feasts, First Communions, and May Crownings—their spiritual lives governed by Catholic school, Mass attendance, and reception of the sacraments—the O'Connors occupied a "meticulously organized world within a world," in the words of biographer Brad Gooch.[3] Savannah Irish Catholics were secure in their role and, in fact, celebrated their religious and ethnic identity each year with a St. Patrick's Day parade that rivaled the annual Confederate Day parade in size and scope. Young Flannery was a part of this rich subculture. As Garry Wills acknowledges regarding the world of his own Catholic boyhood, "It was a ghetto, undeniably. But not a bad ghetto to grow up in."[4]

Mary Flannery, however, was not comfortable with the conformity demanded of children in the world of Catholic school. As the only child of attentive parents—including a particularly doting father—both of whom she addressed by their first names, she was accustomed to spending time in the presence of adults and did not care for the company of children. Edward and Regina enjoyed the stories their daughter told and wrote along with the charming drawings she presented them with. They also encouraged her in her childhood obsession with birds, allowing her to raise them as pets.

One of the imprinting experiences of Mary Flannery's childhood occurred when she was five years old. Pathè News somehow learned of a Georgia child who had achieved the remarkable feat of teaching her pet chicken to walk backwards. The Pathè newsman showed up at the O'Connor home and filmed Flannery and her trick chicken for several hours in the back yard. The fact that they were never able to capture the feat on film—the editor settled for running four seconds of footage film backwards—did nothing to dampen Mary Flannery's enthusiasm for her new-found fame. In O'Connor's words, the event "marked me for life."[5] From that day forward, she began to collect chickens. She had a particular fondness for birds with freakish characteristics, those with mismatched eyes and disproportionate limbs, and searched in vain for those with extra legs and wings. This early focus on so-called "freaks" is portentous. In the stories she would write as an adult, O'Connor would frequently write about people who were "different," who did not fit in, often on account of some sort of physical deformity or limitation. Her fiction presents the reader with a parade of afflicted characters, including one-armed men, one-legged women, club-footed children, women scarred by acne, mentally challenged children, insane adults, and intersex people—all of whose difference place them outside of the norm (for better or for worse). Flannery, in fact, regarded herself as a kind of "freak," a person who did not comfortably fit into any conventional culture she was expected to belong to—and among those cultures she chafed against was that of the institutional church. (This would remain true for all of O'Connor's life, yet her attitude towards the church as a flawed and human institution was generous— she loved it but could not pretend it was perfect.)

It is easy to see why Catholic school might be a trial for an unconventional child. She found the nuns who taught her at St. Vincent's Grammar School for girls to be rigid and unimaginative in their teaching. They faulted her for imperfect spelling and for dwelling on her seeming obsession with ducks and chickens when writing her school themes. Many of the Mercy nuns who taught her were, according to O'Connor, young and exceedingly innocent, just off the boat from Ireland and products of an even more intensely hot-house Catholic culture than the one she knew in Savannah. She took their teachings with more than a grain of salt. One particular story O'Connor relates in her letters in later life illustrates one form her rebellion took: "From 8 to 12 years it was my habit to seclude myself in a locked room every so often and with a fierce (and evil) face, whirl around in a circle with my fists knotted, socking the . . . guardian angel with which the Sisters assured us we were all equipped . . . You couldn't hurt an angel but I would have been happy to know I had dirtied his feathers—I conceived him in feathers."[6]

O'Connor presents the story in comic fashion, but the conflict she felt was serious. Here was a child prepared to do battle with supposed angels who were clearly represen-tations of her own incipient doubts about the teachings being offered her. Even as a child, the theology O'Connor required was far beyond what the relatively unschooled, good sisters could offer.

When Mary Flannery entered the sixth grade, Mrs. O'Connor enrolled her daughter in Sacred Heart School staffed by the sisters of St. Joseph of Carondelet, a more formally educated order of nuns who had, in fact, taught Regina in high school. Moving one's child to a school out-side the parish was unusual, and the gesture was regarded as an attempt on Regina's part to distance her child from the mixed population of shanty and lace-curtain Irish at St. Vincent's and integrate her into the more genteel world of Sacred Heart. Whatever her mother's reasons, Mary Flan-nery was set apart, yet again, from the neighborhood chil-dren. She did seem less troubled in her new school (though she never properly fit in), and the exceedingly bright child of the O'Connors maintained her reputation as a poor speller and an unexceptional, slothful student. (Interestingly, Flannery would remain a self-described "very innocent speller" all her life.)[7]

Exorcising the Self through Fiction

Later in life, O'Connor would write stories that feature children, some of whom share her peculiarities and precociousness. Though they are not strictly autobiographical, some of these characters are surely versions of Mary Flannery's own childhood self. This is certainly true of the unnamed child in "A Temple of the Holy Ghost," an irreverent young girl with a distaste for nuns but a deep-seated spiritual hunger. When her two fourteen-year-old cousins come to visit for the weekend, the twelve-year-old protagonist (an only child) watches them with suspicion. Students at the local convent school, Mount St. Scholastica, they arrive in their brown uniforms calling one another Temple One and Temple Two, a joking reference to advice Sr. Perpetua, an elderly Sister of Mercy, had given her young charges. When importunate boys attempt to make sexual advances, good Catholic girls ought to respond, "Stop sir! I am a Temple of the Holy Ghost!" The girls, who "were practically morons," in the protagonist's estimation, laugh hysterically at this, but the child does not find it funny at all: "I am a Temple of the Holy Ghost, she said to herself, and was pleased with the phrase. It made her feel as if somebody had given her a present."[8] Clearly, the child is oriented toward goodness, hungry for words that convey a vision of the holiness of ordinary, everyday people—yet she is also perverse. Though steeped in religion (she says her prayers and recognizes the *Tantum Ergo* when the girls sing it, jokingly, to scandalize some local Church-of-God boys), she recognizes her sinful nature and her seeming inability to curb it: "She did not steal or murder but she was a born liar and slothful and she sassed her mother and was deliberately ugly to almost everybody. She was eaten up also with the sin of Pride, the worst one." Like many Catholic children, she longs to be a saint, but pondering this one night before falling asleep, she feels her unworthiness: "She could never be a saint, but she thought she could be a martyr if they killed her quick." She then imagines herself being shot, boiled in oil, torn to pieces by lions, and set on fire in cages, trying to decide which fate she could stand. It is difficult for her to know how much she'd be willing to endure for her faith.[9]

The humor in this portrayal is evident—O'Connor knows this child from the inside. Smarter than most people around her, and impatient with the limitations of both her contemporaries and authority figures, Mary Flannery, too, suffered from the sin of pride and was wise enough to know it. (In fact, O'Connor creates a number of characters, adults as well as children, who are afflicted with intellectual pride. She is masterful at getting inside their heads.) As the story continues, we also learn that the child also shares O'Connor's fascination with freaks. When her cousins return from the local fair, she asks them to tell her about what they saw—in fact, she lies to them in order to get them to tell a particularly shocking story of an intersex person who was put on display: "it was a man and woman both. It pulled up its dress and showed us." The young girl wonders at this, but she wonders even more at the message the so-called freak delivers to the spellbound audience: "'God made me this-away . . . . This is the way He wanted me to be and I ain't disputing His way.'"[10] In an intuitive theological leap, the child comes face-to-face with the mystery of the incarnation, the most visible sign of God's unconditional love for his creatures, even in our radical imperfection. She recognizes in the intersex person's public testament of faith an echo of the idea of being a Temple of the Holy Ghost and falls asleep dreaming of the supposed freak as a preacher instructing people in the ways of God.

The story depicts the child's conversion, a new orientation towards holiness, precipitated by this virtual encounter. In the final movement of the story, she accompanies her cousins, along with her mother, when they return to the convent. Kneeling down in the chapel with the students and the nuns, bowing before the monstrance containing the host, hearing the *Tantum Ergo* being sung, "her ugly thoughts stopped and she began to realize that she was in the presence of God. Hep me not to be so mean, she began mechanically. Hep me not to give her so much sass. Hep me not to talk like I do."[11] The child recognizes the Real Presence of Christ—in the Eucharist, in the community, and in herself—and responds with a humility and gratitude we have not seen before. She is also granted a new vision: as they drive away from the convent towards home, she sees the sun, "a huge red ball like an elevated Host drenched in blood, and when it sank out of sight, it left a line in the sky like a red clay road hanging over the trees."[12] Playing on the trope of the sun as Son, O'Connor depicts the child's new understanding of the seemingly ordinary world as visionary, as "charged with the grandeur of God" (in the words of Gerard Manley Hopkins, one of O'Connor's favorite poets), as immanent with divine presence. Thus, the silly cousins, the hapless nuns, and the supposed freak's words all lead the child to her salvation. No one and no thing is beyond redemption. As in all of O'Connor's stories, God works through the corporeal world offering glimpses of the holiness inherent within.

The Way of Sorrow

The great sorrow of Mary Flannery's young life was the death of her father from lupus on February 1, 1941, when she was just shy of sixteen. She made no secret of the fact that he was her favorite parent, and Edward O'Connor did not hide his unconditional love for his daughter. (Regina's love, on the other hand, was deep and sincere, but also tempered with the desire for her child to perform well academically and socially.) What's more, Mary Flannery shared her father's temperament—dreamy (as opposed to practical), artistic (they both loved to draw and to tell stories), and playful (they would create alternate identities for themselves, he "King of Siam" and she "Lord Flannery O'Connor").[13] Later in life, O'Connor would acknowledge, "My father wanted to write but had not the time or money or training or any of the opportunities I have had." In further recognition of their similarities, she notes, "I am never likely to romanticize him because I carry around most of his faults as well as his tastes."[14] Both mother and daughter loved him deeply and were stricken by this loss. In a journal she kept as a young girl, O'Connor wrote these words: "The reality of death has come upon us and a consciousness of the power of God has broken our complacency like a bullet in the side. A sense of the dramatic, of the tragic of the infinite, has descended upon us, filling us with grief, but even above grief, wonder. Our plans were so beautifully laid out, ready to be carried to action, but with magnificent certainty God laid them aside and said, 'You have forgotten—mine?' "[15]

A sense of the fragility of life and the vanity of human wishes becomes a reality for O'Connor, and the young girl's bright future is suddenly shadowed by the inevitability of mortality. This reckoning with reality would inform her personality for the remainder of her days and would become a key aspect of her vision as a writer. For the immediate moment, she realized the direction of their lives would change.

That change, however, had been prepared for in some ways. Beginning in 1932, as the Depression worsened, her father began to experience a series of financial setbacks. When it became increasingly difficult to make a living in the real estate trade as an independent man of business, he sought other opportunities. In 1938, Edward O'Connor was offered a position as senior real estate appraiser for the Federal Housing Administration; however, this good news was accompanied by the unwelcome condition that the family move from the protective environment of their Catholic neighborhood in Savannah to the city of Atlanta. Mary Flannery left Sacred Heart School in March of her seventh-grade year and was enrolled in the parochial school of St. Joseph's Church in Atlanta.

Predictably, perhaps, adjustment to life in the new city proved difficult for mother and daughter, and by the beginning of the fall school term, O'Connor and her mother moved once again, this time to Milledgeville, Regina's hometown, taking up residence in the Cline family mansion. Milledgeville was familiar to Mary Flannery, as she had made many visits there during her childhood to see relatives, but it also presented new challenges and opportunities. Like most small towns in Georgia, it was largely Protestant and had no Catholic schools. O'Connor was enrolled in the Peabody Normal School, an experimental lab school run by the Education Department of the Georgia State College for Women (now Georgia College). For the first time, Mary Flannery found herself outside the bounded world of Catholic school and cultivating friendships with Protestant children. As part of the large Cline clan, there were plenty of family members in her life (all of them adults) and she was still very much a part of a Catholic "ghetto." But she also developed a new sense of herself as being different from her peers on account of her Catholicism—a difference she would gradually own as the meaning and value of her tradition became more evident to her in her new environment.

While Regina and Mary Flannery were living in Milledgeville, Edward O'Connor continued to live and work in Atlanta, coming home on weekends to visit his family. For years he had been suffering from illness, characterized by exhaustion and pain in his joints. Initially misidentified as arthritis, his physicians treated him and he carried on with his work as best he could. Eventually, however, he would be diagnosed with lupus—a disease that mimics arthritis as it attacks the joints, but it causes much greater devastation as the body's immune system attacks its own organs and tissues as well. The O'Connors did not share this diagnosis with their daughter, trying to protect her from the inevitable fear and worry associated with such dire news, but Mary Flannery could not help but notice her father's gradual decline. Even so, when death arrived just one month after his forty-fifth birthday, the family was surprised and stricken. The O'Connors' only consolation was that he was no longer suffering the effects of the dreadful disease that had slowly taken his life. Fortunately, they had no way of knowing that eventually Flannery—who favored her father in so many ways—would suffer the same disease, and that she, too, would die prematurely.

The Road to Recovery

Milledgeville may have been a small town compared with the more cosmopolitan port city of her birth, but, happily, it proved to be a place where Mary Flannery could thrive. A sleepy community of barely six thousand people located at the center of the state, the town had the feel of the Deep South, complete with the provincialism and local color associated with that world.[16] Later on in her life, when O'Connor returned to Milledgeville after her northern sojourn in New York, she would make jokes at the town's expense: "We have a girls' college here," she once wrote to a friend, "but the lacy atmosphere is fortunately destroyed by a reformatory, an insane asylum, and a military school."[17] Once renowned as the largest insane asylum in the world, the Central State Hospital put Milledgeville on the map for Southerners: the expression, "going to Milledgeville," had become code for a person who has lost one's sanity.[18] It was precisely this blend of the genteel and the grotesque that appealed to O'Connor's sensibility. In reality, the countryside surrounding the town was full of grotesques—fake preachers and faith healers, phony Bible salesmen, busybody farmers' wives, Ku Klux clansmen, drifters, and serial killers. These, in fact, are the "freaks and folks" (to borrow a phrase from O'Connor) who would eventually populate her fiction.[19] Thus, Milledgeville was destined to become something more than just a physical home for O'Connor—it would serve as inspiration, ground her imagination, and provide a suitable theater within which her characters could play out the drama of their salvation.

For the time being, though, Milledgeville provided young Mary Flannery with stability, comfortable routine, and an educational system she could rebel against (as was her wont) even as she benefited from it. The Peabody High School O'Connor attended was the antithesis of the rigid Catholic school curriculum she was familiar with. The school offered no classes but featured "activities" in which the course of study seems to have been entirely determined by teachers' whims and students' interests. Instead of studying the periodic table in chemistry, the teacher would ask the students what they wished to learn about and then turn their attention to cosmetics or photography; instead of learning to diagram sentences in English class, they would engage in exercises in literature appreciation; instead of learning about the past in history class, they would report on the headlines in the local paper.[20] None of this took up much of O'Connor's time or attention. Years later she would joke about this exercise in experimental teaching: "I went to a progressive high school where one did not read if one did not wish to. I did not wish to . . ." [21] This is an overstatement, of course—Mary Flannery did read quite a lot. Her particular fascination was the ten-volume commemorative edition of Edgar Allen Poe's work she found on the bookshelf at home. She confesses in the same letter her favorite volume was the *Humorous Tales,* which included absurd stories that appealed to her own offbeat sense of humor. O'Connor recalls, "These were mighty humerous [*sic*]—one about a young man who was too vain to wear his glasses and consequently married his grandmother by accident . . . another about the inmates of a lunatic asylum who take over the establishment and run it to suit themselves."[22] O'Connor shared Poe's penchant for the absurd, and his stories would prove a formative influence on her own vision and voice when she turned her attention to writing.

O'Connor's neglect of her schoolwork also enabled her to dedicate herself to another project she cared deeply about, her role as art editor of the school newspaper, *Peabody Palladium.* In addition to her childhood talents for raising chickens and teaching them to do tricks, Mary Flannery had a gift for comic drawings. Typically, her cartoons were gently satiric commentaries on the culture of high school, allowing her the freedom to be social critic of an institution she also felt at least some small measure of belonging to. (Once again, as in her earlier criticism of nuns and Catholic school, we see O'Connor's seemingly innate distaste for institutions.) Among the most humorous drawings is the one that appeared in the *Palladium* on the day of her graduation, titled "At Long Last . . ." The illustration depicts a girl in a cap and gown rushing with arms extended toward a door marked "EXIT" in large block letters.[23] When Mary Flannery left high school, she was ready.

Preparing for Flight

It may seem surprising that O'Connor chose to remain in Milledgeville and attend Georgia State College for Women (GSCW), but in that time and place (1942 in the rural South), staying close to home was the norm. Nearly all of the girls who graduated from her high school and planned to attend college chose the same route. In addition, Mary Flannery, for all of her mental exuberance and spirit of rebellion, was shy and did not make new friends easily. Finally, she and Regina were still grieving over her father's death the previous year, albeit quietly. Leaving her mother behind to start a new life in a new place did not appeal to her at age seventeen, so instead of moving away, she moved over from the local high school to the local college in the summer just after graduation.

College would supply Mary Flannery some of the intellectual stimulation that high school lacked. She took courses from teachers who recognized and praised her talent as a thinker and a writer—something her previous teachers were reluctant to do, given the seeming oddness of O'Connor's imagination and her unwillingness to conform to boundaries and rules. She formed a number of close friendships with other artistically oriented young women. And in joining the Newman Club, she found a small community of Catholic students (ten altogether, the total number of Roman Catholic students at the college) that met weekly in the Sacred Heart Rectory and attended monthly First Friday Masses together.[24]

O'Connor's college years were heady as well as lively. In December of 1942, the students bore witness to Pearl Harbor, and in January of 1943, the faraway war being waged in Europe came close to home when large groups of WAVES (Women Accepted for Volunteer Emergency Services) arrived in their dorms and classrooms. She also made the acquaintance of a young soldier, Marine Sergeant John Sullivan, stationed at the college naval base. A fellow Irish Catholic, Sullivan became a close friend and visited O'Connor at the Cline family home. She would correspond with him after he was demobilized, but their letters would gradually peter out after Sullivan confided to her his intentions to leave the marines and enter the seminary to study for the priesthood. This is the first of the few romantic relationships O'Connor entered into during her lifetime. Though she was surely disappointed that none of them ended happily, unlike many young women of her place and time, getting married did not rank first on the list of things she hoped to accomplish.

The subject of international politics, as well as local campus events, proved equally welcome fodder for O'Connor's lively imagination, and these show up in her extracurricular work. In her three years at GSCW, O'Connor submitted stories and poems to the college literary magazine, *The Corinthian,* and served as art editor of the college yearbook, *The Spectrum,* to which she contributed linoleum-block cartoons satirizing undergraduate life and the waves of formidable WAVES who dominated the campus scene. She also sent some of her cartoons to *The New Yorker* in the hopes of receiving wider recognition for her work and earning extra income; however, none were accepted. Notably, it is during this period that she begins to sign her academic and creative work as Flannery O'Connor (though family and friends continued to address her as Mary Flannery). The name change, along with the quality of the work O'Connor is producing, suggests a young woman who, if not reinventing herself, was finally coming into her own.

All of this impressed faculty member Dr. George Beiswanger, O'Connor's philosophy professor—so much so that he encouraged Flannery to apply to his alma mater, the University of Iowa. O'Connor leaped at the opportunity, applying to the journalism program in hopes of preparing for a career in newspaper political cartooning. Upon acceptance of her application, she was awarded a journalism scholarship, including full tuition and a stipend of sixty-five dollars per term.

In September of 1945, O'Connor would finally leave Milledgeville, her seven-year sojourn there having come to an end. In his book, *The Life You Save May Be Your Own: An American Pilgrimage,* a joint biography of Dorothy Day, Thomas Merton, Walker Percy, and Flannery O'Connor, Paul Elie identifies this period of O'Connor's life in Milledgeville as crucial. With the death of her father, a man she admired deeply and emulated in any number of ways, O'Connor gradually learned to channel the spirit they shared and assumed the role that he had played—that of the fierce independent. "Independence," Elie argues, "will be the main theme of O'Connor's pilgrimage, in her life and in her fiction."[25] Her creative work gave her confidence in her ability to make her mark in the big world beyond the small town's borders—as well as beyond her region—while her faith equipped her with the necessary courage. As she left for Iowa City to begin her new life, it is likely she believed she was leaving home for good. Little did she know, in just five years' time, she would be returning, and in circumstances no one would have the hardness of heart to intuit or the darkness of mind to imagine.

CHAPTER TWO

Iowa City (1945–48)

Portrait of the Artist as a Young Woman

"I dread, Oh Lord, losing my faith. My mind is not
strong. It is prey to all sorts of intellectual quackery.
I do not want it to be fear which keeps me in the
church . . . I want to love to be in [it]."[1]
—*A Prayer Journal*

The intellectual awakening that had been slowly taking
place during O'Connor's formative years picked up speed
and ran at full throttle during her three years at the University
of Iowa, and it coincided with her discovery of her
vocation as a writer. Within days of her arrival, the young,
formerly shy graduate student made her way to the office
of Paul Engle, director of the legendary Iowa Writers' Workshop,
the first creative writing program to offer a master of
fine arts degree in the United States, and requested entrance
into the program. Engle, taken aback by this unusual request,
made, no less, by a petite teenage girl with a thick

Georgia accent, was unable to understand what she was asking for and requested she write down what she was trying to say: "My name is Flannery O'Connor," she wrote. "I am not a journalist. Can I come to the Writers' Workshop?"[2] Happily, Engle said "yes," enrolled the young woman in two of his courses, and eventually made her his protégé.

Biographer Paul Elie describes O'Connor's discovery as a species of religious revelation: "[The] story of her time there [at Iowa] is not the story of a prodigy amazing the teachers and taking top prizes. It is the story of a conversion to fiction, and then to a certain kind of fiction that was recognizably hers and no one else's."[3] O'Connor began to cultivate her talent for writing with a passion commensurate with only one other pursuit in her life—that of her faith. Perhaps there is little wonder in this as she would come to see the two as so inextricably linked they could not be separated. But before arriving at this understanding of the nexus between her art and her faith, O'Connor would need to struggle with her reasons for writing fiction, its use and value for other human beings, and her hopes and expectations as a writer.

As she wrestled with these difficult questions, O'Connor kept a journal from January of 1946 through September of 1947. In his introduction to her *Prayer Journal*, recently published and made available to readers, William Sessions suggests that O'Connor initiated her journal in response to the "new influences" and "intellectual joys" she was experiencing at Iowa, but also in response to the deep questions and skepticism they engendered in her. Granted, during her time at Iowa, O'Connor attended Mass almost daily, walking to nearby St. Mary's Church, and later would attest that "as soon as I went in the door I was home."[4] She also wrote to her mother every day (as she would continue to do during the next few years when she was living away from her), as another means of maintaining a connection with her past and her identity. But the two lives she was leading—that of a faithful Catholic and that of a student in a secular university characterized largely by a culture of unbelief—were brought into conflict with one another on a daily basis. The journal allowed Flannery space within which to create a "rare colloquy" between the two worlds.[5]

Her fear of losing her faith, articulated in the epigraph to this chapter, was well grounded. Brilliant as she was, O'Connor understood the temptations of the intellect—a recognition evident in her even as a young child. Now, added to this temptation was her ambition to be a writer. We see her wrestling with her pride throughout the journal in passages such as this one: "Dear God, tonight it is not disappointing because you have given me a story. Don't let me ever think, dear God that I was anything but the instrument for your story—just like the typewriter was mine . . . When I think of all I have to be thankful for I wonder that you don't just kill me now because you've done so much for me already and I haven't been particularly grateful."[6]

O'Connor's confession of her ingratitude (eerily reminiscent of the confession of the child in the story "A Temple of the Holy Ghost" quoted in chapter 1), attests to her developing sense of her considerable capacities as a writer and the power exerted on others by her work. With this discovery comes exhilaration, certainly, and joy—but it is also a bit frightening. What is the source of this power? In this particular entry, she seems certain that God, or the Holy Spirit, is responsible for her work, and that she is his instrument. This is consonant with other entries wherein she pleads with God to make her a good writer, to send her a story, to enable her to get her work published, and to enable Christian principles to permeate her work—but very often these entries depict a young woman in a state of desolation, certain of her weakness, ingratitude, and sinfulness. The latter sentiment reaches a climax in the penultimate entry of the journal, dated September 25, 1945: "What I am asking for is really very ridiculous. Oh Lord, I am saying, at present I am a cheese, make me a mystic, immediately."[7]

This plea for a holiness she feels she lacks, written by a twenty-two-year-old in the throes of an ongoing struggle with her faith, is both charming and poignant. O'Connor blends the tragic and the comic in all of her writing, fiction and nonfiction, as it is essential to her vision. Her sense of abandonment is redeemed by her ever-present sense of her own absurdity; her hope that God can and will empower her to be the faithful servant she cannot be on her own attests to her faith. The poignancy of her plea is underscored by the final journal entry, made the following day, in which she concedes defeat in the spiritual battle she has been waging within and against herself: "My thoughts are so far away from God. He may as well not have made me . . . Today I have proved myself a glutton—for Scotch oatmeal cookies and erotic thought. There is nothing left to say of me."[8] Fortunately, O'Connor's prediction of her spiritual demise did not prove true. She would live to fight another day, and her faith would survive the assaults made by her education, both the one received in the writing program at Iowa and the one she would receive in the school of life.

The Education of Flannery O'Connor

O'Connor's experience at Iowa opened up possibilities she had never imagined, in part because of the provincialism of her previous schooling. First, and perhaps most important, she discovered a world of writers she had known nothing about. In a letter to her friend Betty Hester, she confesses,

> I didn't really start to read until I went to Graduate School and then I began to read and write at the same time. When I went to Iowa I had never heard of Faulkner, Kafka, Joyce, much less read them. Then I began to read everything at once, so much so that I didn't have time I suppose to be influenced by any one writer. I read all the Catholic novelists, Mauriac, Bernanos, Bloy, Greene, Waugh; I read all the nuts like Djuna Barnes and Dorothy Richardson and Va. Woolf (unfair to the dear lady, of course); I read the best Southern writers like Faulkner and the Tates, K. A. Porter, Eudora Welty and Peter Taylor; read the Russians, not Tolstoy so much but Dostoevsky, Turgenev, Chekhov and Gogol. I became a Great admirer of Conrad and have read almost all his fiction. I have totally skipped such people as Dreiser, Anderson (except for a few stories) and Thomas Woolf. I have learned something from Hawthorne, Flaubert, Balzac, and something from Kafka, though I have never been able to finish one of his novels. I've read almost all of Henry James. . . . But always the largest thing that looms up is *The Humerous* [sic] *Tales of Edgar Allen Poe.* I am sure he wrote them all while drunk too.[9]

This passage is remarkable for a number of reasons. The scope and breadth of O'Connor's reading is staggering, particularly in the relatively short space of time she accomplished it. (She mentions reading "almost all of Henry James" as a seeming afterthought, whereas given the number, complexity, and length of James's novels, it alone is a considerable feat.) It is also interesting that she begins with "the Catholic novelists," all of whom are European. One of the artistic issues O'Connor is struggling with is learning how to be an *American* Catholic novelist. There are not many models for the kind of writer she hopes to be. (Admittedly, the Tates and Katherine Ann Porter were American Catholics, but they were converts late in life; they possess a self-consciousness about the faith that the cradle-Catholic—who has never known any other way to be in the world other than Catholic—lacks.) Thus, O'Connor's reading served to inspire her, to teach her craft and technique, but it did not overwhelm her with anxiety that she could never measure up. Given the very different project she was up to, she was free to cultivate her own ground and develop her own inimitable style. The same holds true of her reading of Southern novelists, including the larger-than-life Faulkner. Though they shared subject matter, in the broad sense that both were writing about the South, the vision behind O'Connor's fiction was as different as it could possibly be. Her fictional world is one that posits the reality of the incarnation, the Urtext *mythos* of the fall from grace, sin, forgiveness, and redemption.

Another telling aspect of this passage is O'Connor's inclusion of writers whose visions might be characterized as dark. For instance, one can see in the stories that she will write the influence of Hawthorne, who writes morality tales that often incorporate elements of the supernatural and conclude with a shocking turn of events. A case in point would be "Young Goodman Brown," Hawthorne's most celebrated story, wherein a young Puritan's world is rocked after he meets the devil in the forest, attends a satanic worship service where he sees among the participants all of the most virtuous men and women of the town (including his own wife), and upon awakening in the woods (not knowing whether what he had witnessed was reality or a dream) returns home to a life of disillusionment, distrust, and desolation. Many of O'Connor's stories depict encounters with the devil or, at least, some manifestation of profound evil, wherein a seemingly virtuous person must engage in battle for his or her own soul—these include "A Good Man Is Hard to Find" (whose title echoes Hawthorne's) wherein the grandmother meets the Misfit, "Good Country People" wherein Hulga Hopewell meets Manley Pointer, and "The Lame Shall Enter First" wherein Sheppard is duped by Rufus Johnson, among other stories.

O'Connor also includes in her reading list writers who share her own predilection for the macabre and the absurd. Her reading of Kafka's stories, characterized by outrageous and impossible events—the most famous of which is the opening of "The Metamorphosis" wherein the main character awakens to find himself transformed into a giant insect—almost certainly fed her appetite for the ridiculous and the bizarre. It also reflected what she herself saw enacted in Southern culture. The seemingly strange qualities evident in so many of her characters were details O'Connor drew from daily life in the South—O'Connor didn't have to make much up. Finally, the conclusion of her account of her reading with *The Humerous Tales of Edgar Allen Poe*" is vintage O'Connor. Here she is harkening back to home—the reading she did in her room in Milledgeville, borrowing the volume from the Cline family bookshelf. In acknowledging Poe as her earliest influence, she underscores the importance of her formative reading, unsophisticated as it might seem set beside all those seemingly more serious writers, and emphasizes the preeminence of the comic and the grotesque in her aesthetic and imaginative vision.

Mystery and Manners

In addition to all of this reading, O'Connor is writing fiction. As Paul Elie notes in some detail, the six stories that resulted from her Iowa workshop and constituted her master's thesis are apprentice work: "The Coat," The Geranium," "The Turkey," "Wildcat," "The Barber," and "The Crop." The hallmarks of O'Connor's mature fiction—the high comedy, artful dramatic structure, extravagantly barbed metaphor and symbolism—are not yet present. Though O'Connor knows what her material will be—events in the daily life of her Southern characters—she doesn't yet know how to shape that material, to bring it to life. "Something vital is missing from these stories," Elie writes, "They are all manners and no mystery."[10] Elie here refers to a phrase Flannery O'Connor would later coin in an essay "Writing Short Stories" wherein she attempts to describe the elements that go into the mysterious process of creating fiction: "There are two qualities that make fiction," she writes. "One is the sense of mystery and the other is the sense of manners. You get the manners from the texture of existence that surrounds you. The great advantage of being a Southern writer is that we don't have to go anywhere to look for manners; bad or good, we've got them in abundance. We in the South live in a society that is rich in contradiction, rich in irony, rich in contrast, and particularly rich in its speech."[11] From her earliest years, O'Connor possessed a good eye for noticing the visual peculiarities of the world (we need only to recall her penchant for freak chickens) and a well-attuned ear that absorbed the rich idiom of Southern speech. Thus, the "manners" required in good writing came readily to her. In that same essay, she acknowledges the source of difficulty for the beginning writer: "The peculiar problem of the short-story writer is how to make the action he describes reveal as much of the mystery of existence as possible. He has only a short space to do it in and he can't do it by statement. He has to do it by showing, not by saying, and by showing the concrete—so that his problem is really how to make the concrete work double time for him."[12]

It is not surprising, perhaps, that as a twenty-one-year–old trying her hand at fiction for the first time, O'Connor had not yet mastered mystery. This was something that even the fine mentors she had at Iowa could not teach her, for this pursuit was radically bound up with the pursuit of her faith— a faith they did not share. The challenge she faces is as much theological in nature as it is practical and aesthetic—how to incorporate the mystery of the incarnation into her fiction and make it available to an audience that doesn't necessarily understand or believe it. Although O'Connor was not able to articulate this clearly at the time, her journal entries suggest the struggle she will undergo for the next several years as she tries to institute the practice of a Catholic novelist.

As a mature fiction writer, O'Connor reflects on this very topic in another of her essays, "Catholic Novelists." This essay, along with "Writing Short Stories" and a number of other essays, lectures, and critical articles, is published in the aptly named collection *Mystery and Manners*—a tremendous resource for the reader who wishes to understand the relationship between O'Connor's art and her faith. Here O'Connor lays out the *credo* that underlies her own practice as a Catholic novelist: "every mystery that reaches the human mind, except in the final stages of contemplative prayer, does so by way of the senses. Christ didn't redeem us by a direct intellectual act, but became incarnate in human form, and he speaks to us now through the mediation of a visible Church. All this may seem a long way from the subject of fiction, but it is not, for the main concern of the fiction writer is with mystery as it is incarnated in human life."[13]

O'Connor's artistic vision is radically incarnational, in every sense of that word. Her deeply Catholic sense of the world posits belief in the creation as good (albeit misshapen by sin), in the human being as made in the image and likeness of God, and of a world that is immanent with the divine presence. What she will discover, through the practice of her fiction, is a way to harness the meaning inherent in a world already charged with it and make it available to the reader. In order to achieve this tall order, she will need to employ some extreme techniques. These include the use of comedy even (and especially) in tragic circumstances, the use of violence, and the depiction of grotesque and extreme characters. O'Connor explains her rationale behind each of these innovations in her essays. Regarding her love of humor, she reminds us, "Only if we are secure in our beliefs can we see the comical side of the universe."[14] With regard to what she sees as a need for violent action in her plots, she points out that "Violence is strangely capable of returning my characters to reality and preparing them to accept their moment of grace."[15] Finally regarding the presence of the grotesque in her work, O'Connor explains, "When you can assume that your audience holds the same beliefs you do, you can relax a little and use more normal ways of talking to it; when you have to assume that it does not, then you have to make your vision apparent by shock—to the hard of hearing you shout, and for the almost blind you draw large and startling figures."[16]

These signature elements are lacking in O'Connor's first stories as she had not yet found her way to them. Eventually she will, and perhaps the single most instructive writing experience that led her to discover them was the writing of her novel, *Wise Blood,* a project she embarked on in her second year at Iowa in November of 1946. The novel would occupy her time and attention for the next five years. When it was completed, in late 1951, and published on May 15,

1952, *Wise Blood* was as full of mystery and as it was manners, and O'Connor had become the kind of writer she had set out to be.

Mustering Momentum

The Iowa Writers' Workshop proved a boon for O'Connor in a number of ways. In addition to her broad reading and absorbing of literary technique and to gaining practice in her craft, O'Connor earned confidence in her identity as a writer. Though the quality of her work may have been far from what she would produce as a mature writer, it was still very good, even in the competitive atmosphere of Iowa. Her mentors encouraged her to send her work out for publication, and in March of 1946, just before her twenty-first birthday, O'Connor learned that her story "The Geranium" would appear in the summer issue of *Accent*. Having weathered rejections from other journals, this gave O'Connor much-needed confirmation that she had chosen her vocation well. This also distinguished her from her contemporaries in the workshop. She now began to think of herself, in earnest, as a fiction writer.[17] More acceptances would follow; before leaving Iowa, O'Connor would place stories in elite as well as popular journals, including *Sewanee Review* and *Mademoiselle*. Visiting lecturers John Crowe Ransom and Robert Penn Warren, giants in the field of Southern fiction, further boosted O'Connor's confidence when they singled out her stories for commentary and praise. Another mentor and new director of the fiction program, Paul Horgan, taught her the necessity of writing for a set number of hours each day at the same time and without interruption. This habit would become a lifelong practice, one that she would carry out faithfully for the rest of her writing career.[18] Thus,

O'Connor learned discipline and the absolute necessity of taking her work seriously—both things young writers often have difficulty accepting.

Perhaps the most practical benefit O'Connor received from her years at Iowa, in terms of her career as a writer, was the community of writers she had, *de facto*, become a part of. She met influential people who recognized her talent and could advocate for her, and they helped her to navigate the unfamiliar world of writers, grantsmanship, and publishers. When it was suggested that she apply to Yaddo, the artists' colony in Saratoga Springs, New York, she did so and was gratified to be awarded a residency for the summer of 1948. That residency would be extended, and O'Connor would spend a total of nine months in the heady atmosphere of Yaddo, working on her novel and socializing with a revolving group of distinguished and celebrated, if sometimes dysfunctional, writers. When she left Iowa City in June of 1948, her formal education had come to an end, but her education in the writing life was just beginning.

CHAPTER THREE

Northern Sojourn (1948–50)

Wanderer and Wayfarer

"Were it not for my mother, I could easily resolve
not to see Georgia again."[1]
—Letter to Elizabeth Ames, 1948

"The Geranium," the first piece of fiction O'Connor wrote
after arriving at Iowa in 1945, is a story of agonizing homesickness. Dudley, the old man in the story, is a displaced
Southerner who finds himself lost amid the alien culture of
the urban Northeast. He becomes attached to the geranium
on his windowsill, as it reminds him of home, and with
disastrous results. Years later, O'Connor would confess the
tale behind the tale in a letter: "The first story I wrote and
sold was about an old man who went to live in a New York
slum—no experience of mine as far as old men and slums
went, but I did know what it meant to be homesick. I
couldn't though have written a story about *my* being homesick."[2] The last story O'Connor would complete before her
death in 1964, "Judgement Day," is a reworking of her very

first, "The Geranium." The themes of home and displacement, of the conflict of cultures, and of the individual as a stranger in a strange land appear in many of the stories she wrote in between, effectively occupying her for all of her writing life.

As O'Connor suggests in her account of "The Geranium," these stories are as much about her as they are about her invented characters. Yet despite her seemingly permanent state of homesickness, O'Connor did not intend to return to Milledgeville after completion of her MFA—and when she finally did return after being stricken ill, she did so against her will. It was almost as if the home she longed for did not exist. O'Connor had become a sojourner and a self-made exile, and despite her discomfort in this brave new world she traveled, she did not intend to retreat from it until she learned what it had to teach her.

Yaddo

When O'Connor arrived at the Yaddo artist colony in June of 1948—at twenty-three, the youngest and least accomplished of the artists in residence—she had her work cut out for her. The previous year, she had submitted the first four chapters of her novel-in-progress to the Rinehart-Iowa fiction award competition for a first novel and was awarded the $750 prize, with Rinehart holding the option to publish the book upon its completion.[3] Buoyed by this confirmation of the quality of her work, by the promise of publication, and by her admission into the most selective of artist colonies, she arrived determined to make her mark. The experience would be engaging and productive for her. A shy, attractive woman with a quiet presence and a charming accent, O'Connor was well liked by her fellow artists—

so much so she was invited, when her six-week summer residency lapsed—to return for the following fall and spring. By the time she left in February of the following year, she had completed nine chapters of the novel that would make her name.

Though still in a formative stage, *Wise Blood* had begun to take on a life of its own. O'Connor had conceived and created the protagonist, Hazel Motes, a young soldier who returns home from the war only to discover that he doesn't belong there. The world has changed during his absence—as has he—and there is no longer a place for him in the small rural town he emerged from. He then boards a train to the city of Taulkinham, becoming a pilgrim of sorts (not unlike his maker), though unaware of the true destination he is heading for. One of the changes that has taken place in Hazel is that he has lost his faith, or so he believes. Descended from preachers, brought up in a strict evangelical household, Hazel now rejects Jesus and all he has been taught in his church; however, God is not finished with him. As he struggles hard to escape the grip of faith, it will not let him go, provoking in Hazel outrageously defiant behavior that, paradoxically, brings about a conversion in him. Years later, in writing the preface to the second edition of the novel issued in 1962, O'Connor would describe *Wise Blood* this way:

> It is a comic novel about a Christian *malgré lui*, and as such, very serious, for all comic novels that are any good must be about matters of life and death. *Wise Blood* was written by an author congenitally innocent of theory, but one with certain preoccupations. That belief in Christ is to some a matter of life and death has been a stumbling block for some readers who would prefer to think it a matter of no great consequence. For them, Hazel Motes's integrity lies in his trying with such vigor to get rid of the ragged figure who

moves from tree to tree in the back of his mind. For the
author, Hazel's integrity lies in his not being able to do so.[4]

The ragged figure who haunts Hazel is, of course, Christ.
O'Connor's theme is the grace of God, tough as it is tena-
cious, and the redemption available to sinners of every sort
if they are willing to recognize and accept it. Accompanying
Hazel along his spiritual journey is the character of Enoch
Emory, a sort of idiot savant who tries to aid Hazel in his
struggle but doesn't understand the existential agony his
friend is undergoing. Enoch is a dependable source of much
of the novel's dark humor, enabling O'Connor to incorporate
her signature element of comedy in the face of tragedy. Both
the plot and the characters would continue to develop, Hazel
in particular, as O'Connor revised the manuscript over the
next few years, but her months at Yaddo provided her with
the physical and temporal—as well as the mental and spiritual—space she needed to generate creative momentum.

Yaddo also provided her with the gift of literary fellowship. Though she declined to engage in the loose behavior
many of the other artists did—partying, drinking to excess,
and sexual adventures—she enjoyed watching (and com-
menting on) all of this from a studied distance. Her fellow
artists readily recognized that Flannery was different.
Among the things that set her apart was her Catholicism.
When O'Connor first arrived at the colony, she quickly discovered that the only other Catholics present were the men
and women employed to take care of Yaddo's grand gothic
house, its extensive grounds, and its guests. Each Sunday,
she would ride into Saratoga Springs with members of the
staff to attend Mass with them. (Yaddo's distance from the
church forced her to give up the habit of attending daily
Mass she had practiced at Iowa.) In addition, Flannery was

still in avid pursuit of the goal of discovering how to be a Catholic writer; therefore, much of her reading was taken up with books focused on Catholicism. Among these was Jacques Maritain's *Art and Scholasticism,* a philosophical text that would help her to understand the nature of her vocation. Maritain's Thomist definition of art as "a habit of the practical intellect" allowed her to see her role as a crafts-woman, rather than as preacher or teacher of religion or morality. Later in life, in her essay on Catholic novelists, O'Connor would articulate this view of the artist clearly: "St. Thomas Aquinas says . . . that a work of art is a good in itself, and this is a truth that the modern world has largely forgotten. We are not content to stay within our limitations and make something that is simply a good in itself. Now we want to make something that will have utilitarian value. Yet what is good in itself glorifies God because it reflects God. The artist has his hands full and does his duty if he attends to his art. He can safely leave evangelizing to the evangelists."[5]

The Catholic writer should not seek to testify to her faith in the pages of her books or to convert her reader; instead, she should try to write the best fiction that she can. This assurance freed O'Connor to devote herself to "the good" in the form of her craft with the same fervor she devoted to the practice of her religion. She would come to realize that her faith would naturally manifest itself in her art, regardless of the story she might be telling and regardless of whether there was any explicitly Catholic content. This is a key dis-covery for O'Connor, as she had no interest in writing "churchy" stories about priests and nuns, as some of her Catholic contemporaries did. Much as she admired the work of Georges Bernanos, François Mauriac, and J. F. Powers, her experience—and her imagination—was grounded

elsewhere. She wanted to write about the world *she* knew—
that of the American South and the wonderfully strange
people that populated its towns and countryside. What
made a work Catholic was the belief of the artist in a universe "founded on the theological truths of the Faith, but
particularly on three of them which are basic—the Fall, the
Redemption, and the Judgment."[6] This three-part narrative,
the Judeo-Christian *mythos,* is at the heart of every story
O'Connor ever wrote, not because she consciously planted
it there, but because she believed it to be true. If a writer is
Catholic, by her fruits you shall know her.

The sense of being set apart was a familiar sensation to
the girl who had grown up in the Catholic ghetto of Savannah raising freak chickens in the backyard, who never fit in
at Catholic school, who became the new girl in Milledgeville
during the formative period of her adolescence, and who
was one of very few woman—and the rare Catholic—at the
very secular Iowa Writers' Workshop. Not belonging had
become a way of life. Given her sense of isolation, it was a
particular source of pleasure when poet Robert Lowell
showed up at Yaddo in September of 1948. "Cal" Lowell,
already a celebrated poet, having won the Pulitzer Prize the
previous year, was handsome, magnetic, talented, and religious minded. Boston-born, bred from old Puritan stock,
Lowell converted to Catholicism after his first marriage and
shocked a number of his friends and readers. His new-found
faith shaped his poems of the period, but by the time he arrived at Yaddo, he was divorced from his Catholic wife, Jean
Stafford, and no longer practicing the faith. Meeting Flannery changed that. She instantly became his favorite companion and conversationalist, taking obvious pleasure in
listening to her talk about her work. He would attend Mass
with her for the first time in over a year. As biographer Brad

Gooch puts it, "Lowell's feelings were not romantic, but they were full of excitement for her Roman Catholicism and her rare brand of Southern literary talent."[7] Almost certainly due to O'Connor's influence, Lowell gradually returned to the practice of his faith. In a subsequent letter to a friend, she denies being responsible, but clearly rejoices: "I watched him that winter come back into the Church. I had nothing to do with it but of course it was a great joy to me." Given these circumstances, it seems inevitable, perhaps, that O'Connor would develop strong feelings for Lowell, though hers seemed to outstrip his in intensity; eight years later she would confess to a friend, "He is one of the people I love."[8]

Lowell, however, was a troubled soul. His relationship to Catholicism had been passionate but, at times, disordered. Converted largely through his reading of Catholic philosophy and poetry, Lowell was eager to adopt a tradition that set him apart from his Protestant ancestry and his literary contemporaries. Having spent a year in prison as a conscientious objector in 1943, Lowell emerged an ascetic and began a new life wherein he practiced "a penitential regimen of Mass, Benediction, the Rosary, spiritual exercises, a vow of celibacy, and retreats at a Trappist Monastery."[9] All of this stressed his marriage to the breaking point, and by the time he showed up at Yaddo, not only had he left the church, he had begun drinking heavily and was suffering from breaks with reality that would ultimately lead to full-blown psychosis. Finding Flannery, a gifted young writer who was also a member of the Mystical Body of Christ (a doctrine Lowell was especially devoted to as it offered the solitary an opportunity for community), revived his passion for the faith he had abandoned, but it also fueled his tendency towards religious mania. Biographer Paul Elie has suggested that Lowell, in his precarious mental and spiritual state, may have served as an unconscious model for Flannery's Hazel Motes—both were handsome preachers, prophetic in stature, "oracular, puritanical, self-possessed, walking the line between holiness and madness with great poise and eloquence."[10]

Lowell's influence on O'Connor was brief, but would prove to be profound. His confidence in her work, as well as his understanding of her sense of vocation, emboldened her to advocate for herself. When her would-be publisher at Rinehart, John Selby, called for extensive revision of her manuscript of the novel, O'Connor would not capitulate, refusing to render her unconventional novel conventional just to suit an editor or a reading audience. At the same time, another distinguished Yaddo visitor, American literary scholar and critic, Alfred Kazin, came to recognize the genius of the manuscript and recommended it to Robert Giroux at Harcourt Brace. With a potential new editor and publisher waiting in the wings, O'Connor pressed her luck with John Selby and, eventually, freed herself from her contract with Rinehart. Giroux—who had recently published another book by a gifted Catholic writer at the beginning of his career, Thomas Merton's *Seven Storey Mountain*—would end up as publisher of *Wise Blood*.

Lowell would also prove to be O'Connor's accidental means of exit from Yaddo. The politically conservative Lowell (who also had a history of suffering from bouts of paranoia) had grown suspicious of novelist and journalist Agnes Smedley, a personal friend of the director of the colony, Elizabeth Ames, who had been in residence at Yaddo for five years. Both Ames and Smedley had been under FBI investigation as Communist sympathizers, and Smedley had been publicly accused of being a spy, though the accusation had been withdrawn. Nonetheless, Lowell demanded that

Ames be dismissed, and went so far as to conduct a hearing before the Yaddo board in which he examined and cross-examined Yaddo guests (including Flannery) in effort to collect evidence against her. Ultimately, Lowell could not prove the allegations, Ames remained at Yaddo, and he and O'Connor—along with three other writing residents—abruptly departed, setting out for nearby New York City.

Escape to New York

Flannery's flight to New York, in the company of her friends and fellow pilgrims, proved propitious in a number of ways. During her six-month sojourn there, from March through August of 1949, Lowell introduced her to several people who would alter the direction of her life, chief among them Robert Giroux, junior editor at Harcourt Brace who would become her publisher; Robert Fitzgerald, poet, literary critic, and translator of Euripides and Sophocles; and Sally Fitzgerald, aspiring painter who had studied at the Art Students League in New York, and wife of Robert Fitzgerald. All three of them were taken with the quiet young woman who spoke rarely, but did so with a Georgia accent so deep you had to pay perfect attention to understand what she was saying. Flannery was equally taken with them on several counts—for one thing, they were all Catholics. O'Connor found the city of New York—the crush of its nearly eight million souls, its ceaseless activity, and its constant noise—to be overwhelming. The little girl who found it impossible to adapt to living in Atlanta was having no better luck as a young woman in New York. But here, amid a city of strangers, she found a core of people, fellow members of the Mystical Body of Christ, who made her feel less foreign and alone.

When Lowell took O'Connor to meet Robert Giroux in his office at Harcourt Brace on Madison Avenue, she was still contracted to publish her first novel with Rinehart. Giroux had been struck by O'Connor's work—its power and striking originality—and he was equally struck by her: "She was very chary of words . . . But she had electric eyes, very penetrating. She could see right through you, so to speak. I was a young publisher, interested in acquiring writers. I thought, 'This woman is so committed, as a writer, she'll do whatever she's made up her mind to do.' "[11] O'Connor was equally taken by Giroux's work. Before leaving, she made one request of the man whom she would later describe, with characteristic understatement, as "my good editor."[12] She asked for a copy of *The Seven Storey Mountain,* the memoir by Giroux's friend and former classmate at Columbia, Thomas Merton. Giroux had edited and published the story of Merton's conversion to Catholicism and his subsequent abandonment of his literary life in New York in order to become a Trappist monk at Gethsemani Abbey in Kentucky, and the book had become an unlikely runaway best seller. Clearly, Giroux had a genius for recognizing and promoting good Catholic writers, making their countercultural work available and accessible to a vast audience of general readers. As she left the office that day, with Merton's book tucked under her arm, O'Connor did not yet know it, but Giroux would eventually accomplish a similar feat with her work. Though *Wise Blood* would not be an instant best seller—it was too strange for that—it would eventually come to be recognized as one of the classic texts of twentieth century American literature.

O'Connor met Robert and Sally Fitzgerald in their apartment on York Avenue where they lived with their two small children. Robert, a cradle-Catholic from Springfield, Illinois, had left the church briefly, but then returned after leaving his first wife and having his marriage annulled. Sally, the daughter of a Texas judge, had converted to Catholicism and briefly considered joining a convent before her marriage to Robert. The conversation that afternoon was enjoyable, if intense, presided over by Lowell, who was lit up with his new-found religious fervor. Later, O'Connor would describe them as "very intense Catholics" whose "religion colors everything they do."[13] The Fitzgeralds had not read any of O'Connor's work before meeting her, but did so soon afterwards and immediately recognized its power and genius. They would not only become lifelong friends, they would become near family. In a few months' time, the Fitzgeralds would invite Flannery to come to live with them at their new home in rural Connecticut, a large country house purchased to accommodate their growing family. (Eventually, they would have six children.) O'Connor would rent the apartment over the garage where she could write in relative peace and quiet, and spend some time helping to watch over the Fitzgerald children in the afternoons. Living in the woods, far from the madding crowds of New York City, O'Connor would find the conditions she seemed to find necessary for her work to flourish.

Not all of O'Connor's experience in New York, however, was a trial. She eventually settled in an apartment in a rooming house on 108th Street near Broadway on the Upper West Side, not far from Columbia University, with its streets full of students, Jewish families, and recent immigrants to the city, and came to enjoy the neighborhood. Mostly, she worked on her novel, focusing her attention more intently on the internal lives of her invented characters than on the life she herself was engaged in, but she did make some notable exceptions. She attended daily Mass at Ascension Church on 107th, then a largely Irish parish, and enjoyed occasional outings, navigating the complicated system of subways and busses.[14] Her favorite cultural destination was the medieval collection of the Metropolitan Museum of Art at the Cloisters, located high on a hill in northern Manhattan overlooking the Hudson River. The museum, composed of medieval monastic buildings that had been brought to New York from France and Spain, housed (and still houses) a spectacular collection of medieval and Romanesque sculptures and altarpieces, madonnas and crucifixes, and splendidly preserved tapestries and artifacts. In visiting the collection, O'Connor was drawn to a particular object: "I went to the Cloisters twice and I particularly remember one statue that I saw there. As I remember it was about four feet high and on a pedestal. It was the virgin holding the Christ child and both were laughing; not smiling, laughing. I've never seen any models of it anywhere but I was greatly taken with it and should I ever get back to the Cloisters, which is unlikely, I mean to see if it is there."[15]

As she tells this story many years afterwards in 1963, a year before her death, the reader senses a wistfulness in O'Connor's voice. Confined as she is in her rural Georgia home, no longer able to see the image of the madonna in person, she contents herself with revisiting it in her mind's eye. It is also striking that what she loves and recalls most vividly about the image is the laughter of the mother and child. Despite the tragic dimensions of the life Mary and Jesus lived, the vision of the anonymous artist who fashioned the sculpture is governed by what might be termed the Christian comedy. The word *comedy* here is operative in two senses: it suggests humor, a disposition towards joy and an appreciation of the play of paradox that governs human life, and it also suggests the literary term "comedy," a genre wherein circumstances at the beginning of a play that threaten impending disaster are reversed. In a comedy, errors are corrected, offenses are forgiven, and divisions are healed, bringing about unity, amity, and general accord at the end of the drama. Comedy asserts that good can come of evil, and thus serves as a fitting trope for Christian salvation history, wherein the divine plan for human happiness that seemed to be ruined by the fall of Adam and Eve ultimately unfolds, as a result of the redeeming power of the incarnation. Christian comedy asserts that nothing is impossible with God. A comprehensive artistic and theological vision is one that takes this totality into account and sees that tragedy is unfinished comedy to the Christian imagination. This trope has been used by many spiritual writers and poets (perhaps most notably by Dante in his *Divine Comedy*), as well as by the anonymous sculptor, and it is essential to O'Connor's vision as well. O'Connor recognized in this thirteenth-century madonna she happened to come across in New York City a shared sensibility with her medieval brother and a timeless truth; no wonder she treasured the memory of it for the rest of her life.

Before leaving New York, O'Connor also learned firsthand the degree to which the practice of Catholicism was countercultural in the context of the mainstream literary establishment. Another celebrated person Lowell introduced her to was Mary McCarthy, novelist and "big intellectual" in Flannery's words, who had been raised Catholic but had rejected the faith in her teens. McCarthy would famously record her de-conversion story in *Memories of My Catholic Girlhood*, thus making herself a Catholic writer of a very different stamp. The night O'Connor arrived for dinner at the midtown apartment where McCarthy lived with her husband, Bowden Broadwater, Lowell was particularly talkative (in truth, he was entering one of his manic phases).

McCarthy and Broadwater gave as good as they got, and Flannery had some difficulty keeping up with the dizzying pace of the conversation. A moment did arrive, however, at about 1:00 a.m., when she could not hold her tongue. O'Connor would tell the story years later in a letter to her friend, Elizabeth Hester: "Well, toward the morning, the conversation turned on the Eucharist, which I, being the Catholic, was obviously supposed to defend. Mrs. Broadwater said when she was a child and received the Host, she thought of it as the Holy Ghost, He being the "most portable" person of the Trinity; now she thought of it as a symbol and implied that it was a pretty good one. I then said, in a very shaky voice, "Well, if it's a symbol, to hell with it."[16]

O'Connor's rejection of McCarthy's condescension is striking, as well as characteristic of her. While she was content to sit and listen to the literary talk, much of which she may have disagreed with, when it came to Catholic doctrine, she felt compelled to bear witness to this central truth of her faith—belief in the transubstantiation of bread and wine into the body and blood of Christ.

In fact, the Real Presence of Christ in the Eucharist was an article of absolute faith for O'Connor: in her words, "it is the center of existence for me; all the rest of life is expendable."[17] Her belief is also part and parcel of her vision as a Catholic writer. In every one of her stories, the central character is, in some way, brought face-to-face with the presence of the divine in the physical world, even in the most mundane aspects of creation. This vision is shared and expressed by the narrators, bodied forth in details great and small, and permeates her fiction. In her story, "A Good Man Is Hard to Find," as the family is driving through the countryside on their way to their vacation and the impatient children are complaining about the length of the journey, young

John Wesley says, "Let's go through Georgia fast so we won't have to look at it much." As if in counterpoint to his contempt for the world he inhabits, the narrator quietly observes, "The trees were full of silver-white sunlight and the meanest of them sparkled."[18] Even in a detail as small and as subtle as this, the message is clear: the seemingly ordinary world is, in reality, a beatific vision when seen through the eyes of faith, as it bodies forth the beauty of its creator. God's Real Presence is evident everywhere.

Flannery O'Connor's adult life might be seen as a succession of intense friendships. In befriending her and introducing her to influential people, Robert Lowell had proven a loyal and much-loved presence; thus, it was heartbreaking to Flannery when he suffered a complete mental breakdown shortly after his religious conversion. His religious obsession was characterized by visions and delusions, during one of which he envisioned O'Connor as a saint. One day he called Robert Fitzgerald to share news of his re-conversion: that on March 2, Ash Wednesday and his birthday, he had "received the shock of the eternal word" while immersed in a freezing bath on his hands and knees gasping prayers to Therese of Lisieux. He went on to announce that today (March 4) "is the day of Flannery O'Connor, whose patron saint is St. Therese of Lisieux."[19] Talk of Lowell's visions and of his canonization of O'Connor spread among the Manhattan literati, engendering pity and embarrassment on his behalf among his friends. Soon after, Lowell was institutionalized and underwent electroshock therapy. When he emerged, his faith was gone. Later, O'Connor would express her sorrow at these events: "I feel almost too much about him to be able to get to the heart of it. He is a kind of grief to me . . . There is a part of me that won't be at peace until he is at peace in the Church." At the time, Flannery did not recognize Lowell's behavior as a form of madness—"I was only 23 and didn't have much sense"[20]—but she also knew this was no ordinary devotion. In the fiction she would write in subsequent years, O'Connor would portray characters afflicted by religious mania with great compassion, chief among them the main character in the novel she had been working on at Yaddo, in New York City, and would continue to work on in Connecticut—Hazel Motes.

Escape from New York

On September 1, 1949, O'Connor moved into her writer's garret over the attached garage at Robert and Sally Fitzgerald's house in Ridgefield, Connecticut. The distance from the Upper West Side of Manhattan to 70 Acre Road was no more than two hours, but her new home seemed a world away. "Me and Enoch are living in the woods in Connecticut with the Robert Fitzgeralds," Flannery wrote to a friend, betraying the degree to which her fictional characters tended to take on a life of their own, making them as vivid and present to her as her flesh-and-blood friends.[21] In the course of her sixteen-month sojourn in the woods, Flannery would bring her novel to near completion, sign a contract with her new publisher, and develop a deep and abiding friendship with the Fitzgerald family that would last the rest of her life. They were, in many ways, the happiest months of her life.

O'Connor's new routine was as regular as it is enviable as a model for a writer's—and, particularly, a Catholic writer's—life. She rose early to attend Mass at Sacred Heart Church in Georgetown (four miles away) with one of the Fitzgeralds, ate breakfast with the family, and then retired to the blissful quiet of her apartment to work for four hours on her novel. At noon, she would eat lunch and walk the half-mile to the mailbox to post her daily letter to her mother (a practice O'Connor observed religiously all of the years she lived apart from Regina). In the afternoon, she would help oversee the Fitzgerald children. As one might suspect, Flannery made for an unorthodox babysitter. Sally Fitzgerald recalled an episode that typified her style of child rearing that might be characterized as benign neglect: "Flannery would lie on the bed and watch the child as she would play around the room. I remember once she told me that she listened to her howling . . . and finally, when she paused for breath, Flannery said, 'Your mom can't hear you over here.' The child waited, then walked over to the door and started howling out, which Flannery reported to us."[22] At the end of the day, when the children were in bed and Robert returned from his day of teaching at Sarah Lawrence in Westchester County, the adults would mix a pitcher of martinis, share an evening meal, and talk late into the night about their common passions—literature and religion.

O'Connor treasured these conversations. They were as literary as any she had experienced at Yaddo, but the added dimension of bringing Catholic writers into the conversation grounded their love of books and their practice as writers in their faith. They circulated books by Lord Acton, the Catholic historian, John Henry Newman, and Fr. Philip Hughes, whose history of the Reformation in England O'Connor much admired. In addition, Robert Fitzgerald shared Flannery's conviction that good literature fed the soul as surely as it fed the heart and the mind. They shared their favorite books and authors—Flannery suggested that they read books by Southern writers, such as William Faulkner's *As I Lay Dying*, and Robert gave Flannery drafts of his working translation of *Oedipus Rex*, a play she had not yet read and whose terrifying conclusion would inspire her to reshape the events of

Wise Blood. In what is perhaps the book's most harrowing scene, Hazel Motes blinds himself with quicklime, one of several penitential acts he performs towards the end of the novel. The deed is an echo of the failed attempt at self-blinding on the part of the false prophet (and Motes's nemesis), Asa Hawks, only Motes succeeds, effectively discrediting his rival. The action, at first glance, might seem as random as it is shocking and horrifying, yet seen as a corollary to Oedipus's blinding of himself, the reader comes to recognize it for the brilliant trope that it is—Motes enacting both Oedipus's and his own recognition of his primal sin, its irrevocable nature, and his near despair.

Clearly, all of this conversation, in addition to her reading, fueled and fired O'Connor's writing, deepening her vision and enabling her to work at an unaccustomed pace: "The novel is going well, almost fast," Flannery—a famously slow and deliberate writer—wrote to a friend.[23] O'Connor seemed to have found the ideal life among friends and fellow members of the Mystical Body of Christ. As time passed, their relationship would further deepen. In May of the following year, Flannery stood as godmother to the Fitzgeralds' third child, Maria Juliana, along with the infant's godfather, Robert Giroux. "She was now one of the family," Robert Fitzgerald observed, "and no doubt the coolest and funniest one."[24] The young woman who had arrived at Yaddo just two years earlier, a friendless stranger, must have felt as if she had, at last, found the home she had been searching for.

In December of 1950, Flannery O'Connor boarded a train bound for Georgia to visit her mother for the Christmas holidays. Prior to her journey, she had been feeling poorly, complaining to the Fitzgeralds of a heaviness in her arms that made the work of typing her novel difficult. The Fitzgerald family physician diagnosed her joint pains as arthritis, but urged her to go to the local hospital in Milledgeville for a complete physical during her visit. Flannery seemed well as she boarded the train, despite a touch of stiffness Sally noticed in her gait. The two women said their farewells, looking forward already to their reunion in January—but no such reunion would take place. By the time the overnight train reached its destination, Flannery was desperately ill. Her Uncle Louis, who picked her up at the station, was shocked to see his young niece hobble off the train looking like "a shriveled old woman."[25] He drove her straight to Baldwin General Hospital. Within days, the diagnosis would be clear: Flannery was dying of lupus, the disease that killed her father and would, over the next thirteen years, slowly kill her. She would not be returning to live with her new-found family, to enjoy Mass and martinis and literary conversation, or to write in her garret above the Fitzgeralds' garage. O'Connor had gone back to Georgia for good.

CHAPTER FOUR

Return to Milledgeville (1951–53)
The Country of Sickness

> "I have never been anywhere but sick. In a sense, sickness is a place, more instructive than a long trip to Europe, and it's always a place where there's no company; where nobody can follow. Sickness before death is a very appropriate thing and I think those who don't have it miss one of God's mercies."[1]
> —Letter to Betty Hester, 1956

Flannery O'Connor's train ride took her back to the world she had known, but it also transported her to a new place—the country of sickness, a world utterly governed by the body. For the remainder of her life, she would be subject to its severe demands and its heartbreaking frailties. In addition to being a brutal disease, lupus is wildly unpredictable as it manifests differently in every patient. Flannery's lupus would not look like her father's—it would prove much more virulent and incapacitating. She would suffer dangerously high fevers, rampant infections, necrosis of the jaw, which would make eating an ordeal, and deterioration of her joints, hip-bone, and skeletal muscles—so much so that she would need to use crutches to move about. To worsen matters, O'Connor's physical deterioration would be aided and abetted by the drugs she was given to control the lupus. Her daily high doses of the corticosteroid ACTH (administered through injections she would learn to give herself) would provide some temporary relief of her symptoms, but they weakened her bones, thinned her hair, and caused swelling, creating a moon-face effect that embarrassed her. In most of the photographs taken of O'Connor after her diagnosis, she appears aged beyond her years and bears little resemblance to the pretty young woman who went off to Iowa just a few short years before.

But Flannery was also a fighter. Not only would she learn to live with her disease, she would learn to find grace in it, eventually counting her affliction as "one of God's mercies." In her letters, she describes with patience, wit, and good humor the gradual diminishment of her physical capacities. At the age of twenty-five, when most young people are still laboring under the delusion that they are immortal, O'Connor looked her mortality in the face every day, and this gave her strength and purpose. Throughout the ordeal of her illness, she poured herself into her writing, refusing to give up her vocation regardless of the precious energy it cost her. It is no accident that her stories are filled with characters who suffer physical, mental, and spiritual limitations—missing limbs, poor eyesight, mental handicaps, deafness, and muteness—and that these afflictions lead to their salvation and the salvation of others. This, of course, is classic Catholic and Christian theology, only O'Connor was not merely *writing* about the cross—the pattern of suffering that leads to redemption—she was living it.

Crisis and Recovery

O'Connor survived the fierce onset of the disease she suffered on the train. She spent Christmas in the Milledgeville hospital, where the doctors concurred with the diagnosis of rheumatoid arthritis, but Flannery's raging fevers persisted, and she was eventually moved to Emory University Hospital in Atlanta where the diagnosis of lupus was confirmed. Her mother was horrified at this news and would not allow the doctors to inform Flannery, believing it would be devastating for her to learn she had the disease that had slowly and cruelly killed her father. Needing to share the burden with someone, Regina informed Sally Fitzgerald of Flannery's true condition, while she chose to let her daughter live with the fiction that she had arthritis.

Seventeen months later, on a summer visit in 1952 with the Fitzgeralds, O'Connor would finally learn the truth from Sally. Brad Gooch relates Sally's recollection of the fateful moment: "Reacting to this sudden revelation, Flannery slowly moved her arm from the car door down into her lap, her hand visibly trembling . . . . 'Well, that's not good news,' Flannery said, after a few silent, charged moments. 'But I can't thank you enough for telling me. . . . I thought I had lupus, and I thought I was going crazy. I'd a lot rather be sick than crazy.' "[2] Though Regina might have spared O'Connor the sensation of going crazy, she did, in fact, give her daughter the gift of time—time to gradually adjust to the new country she had arrived at. As her daughter was enduring her first bout with what she thought was arthritis, she was hopeful of her eventual recovery. Believing she would be returning to her literary life in New York and Connecticut undoubtedly gave her the strength and drive to get well, both during her eight months in the Atlanta hospital and beyond. It also enabled her to stay focused on her work—and work she did. Gravely ill, O'Connor essentially finished her novel as she lay on what might well have proven her deathbed.

In a letter to a friend, Flannery describes the almost manic state she was in as she revised the final chapters of *Wise Blood*:

> I was five years writing that book, and up to the last I was sure it was a failure and didn't work. When it was finished I came down with my energy-depriving ailment and began to take cortisone in large doses and cortisone makes you think night and day until I supposed the mind dies of exhaustion if you are not rescued. I was, but during this time I was more or less living my life and H. Mote's too and as my disease affected the joints, I conceived the notion that I would eventually become paralyzed and was going blind and that in the book I had spelled out my own course, or that in the illness I had spelled out the book.[3]

Fueled by steroids, O'Connor experienced the ferocious energy necessary for her to rewrite the story (in longhand, no less) she had labored at so long, but she also experienced the strange sensation of identifying with her obsessed, Christ-haunted, and borderline pathological protagonist, Hazel Motes. Both the creator and her creature were undergoing a baptism by fire, both in physical and spiritual terms, suffering the privations and desolations that, paradoxically, bring one to faith. O'Connor poured into her novel all of her own agonies—not only her disease, but also her displacement. As Paul Elie has observed, "Coming home for O'Connor was a crucifixion, with all the term implies. In her illness, and the loneliness it brought, she saw the suffering of Christ, whose suffering was the model for the suffering of Hazel Motes."[4] Eventually, Hazel would emerge not only saved, but a saint. O'Connor would emerge chastened, reconverted to her own faith, and grateful to be alive.

The Kingdom of Andalusia

When O'Connor came home from the hospital, she had difficulty walking, and the Cline mansion in Milledgeville, with its many stairs, proved difficult for her to navigate. It was decided that she and Regina would move to the family dairy farm located five miles outside of town. A true working farm, Regina would run the place, and Flannery would write and recuperate. Their only steady company would be fellow dairymen, the occasional deliveryman, and the African-American farmhands that lived and worked on the property. They set up a room on the ground floor that would serve as Flannery's bedroom and writing studio. Though a far distance from her garret in the north woods, the view from this room of her own was similar. Outside she could see trees and sky, only they were Georgia trees—pin oak and pine—and the sky was wide. She was not in Connecticut anymore. Flannery rechristened the farm "Andalusia," a name that had fallen out of usage but she chose to resurrect. There is a power in naming things, and O'Connor was tapping into that power. As Paul Elie astutely observes, "The farm would be what she made of it. She would claim it as her own."[5] This was the first of many acts of reinvention Flannery would engage in; if she were going to endure exile, it would be on her terms.

In the years to come, she would make her mark on the farm in many other ways, perhaps most notably by introducing peacocks into her new realm. In the summer of 1952, she would order a pair of peafowl and four peachicks. The little girl who raised common (and uncommon) chickens in Savannah and Milledgeville had graduated to connoisseur of that magnificent bird, the peacock. The original pair and their four offspring would quickly grow into a large herd of forty or so, dominating the small farm, eating Regina's flowers, roosting in the low-branched trees, and letting loose with their raucous calls. In her essay "The King of the Birds," O'Connor describes the earthy, yet unearthly, quality of the creature's voice: the peacock "appears to receive through his feet some shock from the center of the earth, which travels upward through him and is released: *Eee-ooo-ii! Eee-ooo-ii!* To the melancholy this sound is melancholy and to the hysterical it is hysterical. To me it has always sounded like a cheer for an invisible parade."[6] To ordinary ears, the peacocks' cries were mostly a source of annoyance—but, clearly, Flannery heard something different in their uniquely strange and strident voices. It was as if each cry were an annunciation.

Most of O'Connor's admiration for the bird, however, was focused on its tail. The peacock does not fan his magnificent feathers for everyone. It is an occasion that must be waited for with patience, and when it does occur, observed with reverence and awe. In her essay, she describes the experience the viewer receives as nothing short of visionary: "When it suits him, the peacock will face you. Then you will see in a green-bronze arch around him a galaxy of gazing, haloed suns."[7] The peacock is a creature that has long been charged with theological significance. The "suns" she refers to, the lovely golden glow in the center of each feather, are reminiscent of the "son" at the center of the Christian universe. In the medieval church, the peacock is frequently used as a symbol of the resurrection and the second coming, the saving and transformative presence of Christ in the world. Those circular centers also resemble eyes, "gazing" at the watcher. As O'Connor points out in one of her letters, the peacock "also stands in medieval symbology for the Church—the eyes are the eyes of the Church."[8] Given these associations, there is little wonder O'Connor chose it as her signature bird.

Not surprisingly, peacocks also appear in O'Connor's fiction, and when they do, they carry a great weight of meaning. In her story "The Displaced Person," the peacock on Mrs. McIntyre's farm makes several appearances at key points in the story. In the beginning, we see Mrs. Shortley, a character who lacks the ability to see things as they are, walk up a hill to survey the surrounding countryside. She does not know it, but she is being followed: "The peacock stopped just behind her, his tail—glittering green-gold and blue in the sunlight . . . flowed out on either side like a floating train and his head on the long blue reed-like neck was drawn back as if his attention were fixed in the distance on something no one else could see."[9] As the events of the ensuing story demonstrate, unlike the peacock's, Mrs. Shortley's vision is flawed and partial. What she doesn't foresee is the arrival of the Displaced Person, Mr. Guizac, whose incursion into the farm community will ultimately displace everyone, including her. The difference between her and the peacock is that she mistakenly believes her vision is comprehensive and penetrating. The peacock is guilty of no such presumption. As it turns out, Mrs. Shortley's lack of vision, lack of humility, and, ultimately, lack of charity will cost her dearly.

Later on in the story, the creature makes another appearance. Old Fr. Flynn, the priest who brings the Guizac family to the farm, giving them the opportunity for employment and Mrs. McIntyre the opportunity to help out her fellow man, is especially taken with the peacock. While she believes the birds to be a nuisance, he sees them as nothing short of miraculous. As Mrs. McIntyre is complaining to him about the Displaced Person, whose innocent presence has upset the (mostly envious) workers on her farm, he is distracted by the vision of the peacock raising its tail: "The cock . . . raised his tail and spread it with a shimmering timbrous noise. Tiers of small pregnant suns floated in a green-gold haze over his head. The priest stood transfixed, his jaw slack. Mrs. McIntyre wondered where she had ever seen such an idiotic old man. 'Christ will come like that!' he said in a loud gay voice and wiped his hand over his mouth and stood there, gaping."[10] The priest's instinctive identification of the bird with Christ at this crucial moment in the story—and Mrs. McIntyre's inability to appreciate the miracle that appears before her—is an indication of her spiritual blindness. The priest's vision is thoroughly Catholic—he sees God in the world, evidenced among his creatures, both human and non-human. Mrs. McIntyre, on the other hand, is a practical property owner. She doesn't have a visionary bone in her body. She does not see the divinity in the peacock—or in the priest—or in the Displaced Person—or in her other work-ers—or in herself, for that matter. Like Mrs. Shortley, she, too, will suffer as a result of this lack of vision. O'Connor grounds the theological concept of immanence in the con-crete presence of the peacock, which serves at one and the same time as ordinary bird and yet symbol and sign.

The story of "The Displaced Person" is clearly set in a place that is similar to Andalusia. Not only are the peacocks present, the plot is based on actual events. In August of 1953, a family of Polish refugees arrived to work on Regina's farm. O'Connor observed them and chose to make them the cen-ter of her story (though she took considerable liberties with the plot as the actual refugee family did not suffer the tragic fate the fictional Guizacs do). By December, O'Connor wrote the story, read it aloud to a gathering of literary friends, and later submitted it for publication to *Sewanee Review*. This would be one of many such instances, where the stuff of O'Connor's daily life would become the stuff of her art. They say that truth is stranger than fiction—a fact that is nowhere more true than in the American South. Andalusia may have been far from the literary action of New York City, but, as O'Connor would discover, there was plenty of human action to compensate for this seeming deficit.

Launching a Career from Afar

On May 15, 1952, *Wise Blood* was finally published. After five years of laboring over the manuscript, including her "deathbed" revisions, Flannery sent it off to her friend and trusted reader, Robert Fitzgerald. At his suggestion, she also sent it off to novelist and critic, Caroline Gordon, for review. Married to poet and influential critic, Alan Tate, both he and Gordon were converts to Catholicism and in search of a Catholic literary "Renascence."[11] Gordon gave O'Connor many useful suggestions for revision, but, in general, was thrilled with the novel: "This girl is a real novelist," she wrote to Fitzgerald, "already a rare phenomenon: a Catholic novelist with a real dramatic sense, one who relies more on her technique than on her piety."[12] O'Connor, always humble before her art, was eager to incorporate Gordon's revisions, many of which taught her lessons about fiction writing that would help her shape her stories for years to come. Thus, the two writers became friends and confidantes.

With all of the revisions complete, O'Connor sent the final manuscript to Robert Giroux, friend and fellow

Catholic (like Fitzgerald and Gordon) who had believed in and supported her project from the beginning. As Paul Elie demonstrates so compellingly, this small circle of people—in addition to some others closely associated with them, including Robert Fitzgerald, Robert Lowell, Alan Tate, Thomas Merton, Dorothy Day, and Walker Percy—constituted, if not a Catholic literary revival, a Catholic movement in America, albeit an accidental one. This unconscious community of like-minded artists trying to figure out how to write about belief in an era of unbelief, constituted, in Gordon's words "The School of the Holy Ghost."[13] Young Flannery was at the center of this movement and, though the youngest among them, would arguably become the most celebrated and successful. *Wise Blood* marked the beginning of a brilliant career—not only as a Catholic writer, or an American writer, or even as a Southern writer—but as a writer who transcended all of those categories even as she worked within the limitations each imposed.

Flannery's concerns, however, were much less lofty. *Wise Blood* was such a thoroughly unconventional novel, it was widely misunderstood—both by critical readers accustomed to literary fiction and by locals. Upon the book's release, O'Connor had to endure a round of celebrations in Milledgeville, including an autograph party at her alma mater, the Georgia State College for Women (GSCW). It amused her to imagine what all of these proper Southern ladies would think when they took home the novel they were purchasing with such enthusiasm. She didn't have to wait long to find out. In Brad Gooch's amusing account of some of the local reactions, several stand out. Flannery's first college writing teacher, upon reading the description of Mrs. Watts (the prostitute Hazel visits when he first arrives in Taulkinham) as she lounges in her place of business—"the friendliest bed in town"—flung the book across the room. Later, in an interview, Miss Scott opined (with a wry Southern wit not unlike Flannery's), "When I read her first novel I thought to myself that character who dies in the last chapter could have done the world a great favor by dying in the first chapter instead."[14] Though Flannery disliked the publication parties, she did appreciate the invitations extended to her to offer lectures and author talks from GSCW and other such schools. Flannery would make many such appearances in the years to come, giving her the opportunity to expound on her craft as a fiction writer, her identity as a Catholic writer, and the theological vision that informs her art. These were occasions for her to articulate her own thinking and also to clear up some misapprehensions about her work. For instance, the students at GSCW associated O'Connor's work with the existentialist philosophies of Kafka and Kierkegaard—an erroneous connection that was common in academic and critical circles as well. Flannery was glad to correct them, explaining that her real debts were owed to the writings of the saints and to Catholic theologians, such as Thomas Aquinas. As she would later quip, "Everybody who has read *Wise Blood* thinks I'm a hillbilly nihilist, whereas I would like to create the impression . . . that I am a hillbilly Thomist."[15]

This dichotomy will show up in a number of O'Connor's stories in the years to come. Characters who believe in nothing (or at least think they do), such as the Misfit in "A Good Man Is Hard to Find" and Manley Pointer in "Good Country People," are thrust into conflict with characters who do believe in God and in an ordered universe, despite the doubts or misconceptions they might harbor. The two extremes are combined in Hazel Motes, who in his attempt to found the church without Christ, starts out by denying Christ and the meaning his existence imposes upon the universe, but ends up embracing the most radical imitation of Christ, including self-sacrifice and self-annihilation. His practice is lurid, extreme, and violent, manifested by his self-blinding, the wearing of barbed wire as a penitential garment, and filling his boots with nails and glass—but these are not the actions of a man who believes in nothing. Quite the contrary—a man deeply aware of his sins, the most heinous of which is the murder of an innocent man whom he took to be mocking him—Hazel is seeking redemption, trying to save his immortal soul.

In her essay "Catholic Novelists and Their Readers," O'Connor explains the method behind her seeming madness, accentuating (again) the necessity of violence. Because "we live in a world that since the sixteenth century has been increasingly dominated by secular thought, the Catholic writer often finds himself writing in and for a world that is unprepared and unwilling to see the meaning of life as he sees it. This means frequently that he may resort to violent literary means to get his vision across to a hostile audience, and the images and actions he creates may seem distorted and exaggerated to the Catholic mind."[16] Caroline Gordon understood and admired O'Connor's literary credo. She recognized the supposed "freaks" in O'Connor's work that mystified some reviewers as exaggerated expressions of flawed humanity. Nonetheless, once she finished *Wise Blood*, Flannery confided to Gordon that she would move in a different direction and focus on writing about "folks" instead of "freaks."[17] O'Connor stayed true to her word—after a fashion. She became an avid observer of her circumscribed world. With her eye for detail and with her fine ear for idiom, she watched and listened to her neighbors, including the Stevens family—her mother's dairyman, his wife, and two daughters, who would provide models for her of the white sharecroppers featured in her stories—and would capture images, expressions, and snippets of speech that would later find their way into her narrative and dialogue. She would also study the town newspapers for interesting local stories, scenarios, and names of characters.[18] O'Connor discovered in the sleepy Georgia countryside a world full of folks who would populate the world of her fiction. As a result of this new vision, she would experience a surge in her literary productivity, writing three new stories ("The Life You Save May Be Your Own," "A Late Encounter with the Enemy," and "The River") and beginning a second novel (*The Violent Bear It Away*)—in addition to finishing and publishing her first novel—all within eighteen months of her release from the hospital. Later in life, O'Connor will acknowledge in a letter the grace of both her return to the South and even the horrific illness that occasioned it: "I stayed away from the time I was twenty until I was twenty-five with the notion that the life of my writing depended on my staying away. I would certainly have persisted in that delusion had I not got very ill and had to come home. The best of my writing has been done here."[19] Though she may have been dragged back to Georgia kicking and screaming, Flannery found there what she had been searching for all along.

CHAPTER FIVE

Freaks & Folks (1954–55)

"Good Country People"

"If you believe in the divinity of Christ, you have to cherish the world at the same time that you struggle to endure it."[1]

— Letter to Betty Hester, 1955

While it's true that Flannery's life at Andalusia was circumscribed, she did make occasional forays into the outside world, and people from the outside world came to visit her. She was not unlike a religious who takes a vow of stability, swearing loyalty to a particular place, but escaping its confines on occasion to get a broader view of the humanity she has devoted herself to praying for—or in O'Connor's case—writing about.

Her trip to Connecticut in 1952 to visit the Fitzgeralds for five weeks had delighted her. It also delighted the Fitzgerald children, as she smuggled three live ducklings on the plane as gifts for them.[2] But the contact with the outside world had also made her sick, forcing her to return home abruptly. It was during this visit that she learned from Sally the true nature of her disease, and a virus (likely caught from one of the four Fitzgerald offspring she was minding) reawakened her lupus with a vengeance. On her return to Georgia, she had to undergo two blood transfusions and spent six weeks in bed. Up until now, Flannery had assumed she would be able to return to her old life. Sally's revelation—and the evidence of her body's fragility—put an end to any such illusions. As if in recognition of the new dispensation, she sent for the few clothes and books she had left behind at the Fitzgeralds.

She did, however, receive some consoling news. Encouraged by influential writer and critic, John Crowe Ransom (whom she had met at Iowa), to apply for the new *Kenyon Review* fellowship on the strength of her powerful first novel, Flannery did so. In December of that year she learned that she won the $2,000 grant. She would use it to pay for her blood transfusions, her ACTH meds, and some books she had been wanting. Regina was much taken with her daughter's success, now measureable in practical terms. Winning money for her writing seemed to legitimize her stories in ways nothing else could, to Regina's mind, while for Flannery, the confirmation of the worth of her work could not have come at a better time. Happily, it would be the first of many such awards O'Connor would garner—both monetary and honorary—for her fiction. Strangely enough, just as Flannery was growing less capable of going out into the world, it seemed to be coming to her.

"The World Is Almost Rotten"

Another honor O'Connor garnered was second prize in the O. Henry Awards the following year for "The Life You

Save May Be Your Own." This story about a shiftless wanderer named Tom T. Shiftlet and his arrival on the farm owned by Lucynell Crater, which she occupies with her mute and mentally handicapped daughter (also named Lucynell), serves as a magnificent example of O'Connor's mining of the local in order to tell a mythic tale. It also demonstrates her deep engagement with theological ideas that put forth her Catholic world view.

Originally entitled "The World Is Almost Rotten," echoing the sentiment expressed by Mr. Shiftlet when he first arrives at the Crater farm, the story portrays the battle of wills between the scheming lady farmer (who was "ravenous for a son-in-law") and the scheming Mr. Shiftlet, who has designs on her 1928 Ford.[3] Both characters are flawed in their ways, but Shiftlet bears the marks of one of O'Connor's afflicted. He is missing half of his left arm, a sign that he is not whole, neither physically nor spiritually. Mrs. Crater, on the other hand, is a monumental woman, huge and powerful, watching the sunset along with Shiftlet as if she owns it. Accompanying these two formidable presences, both of whom are accustomed to manipulating others to achieve their own ends, is the daughter Lucynell. Oblivious to their machinations, she watches with intensity, if not understanding, "her head thrust forward and her fat helpless hands hanging at the wrists. She had long pink-gold hair and eyes as blue as a peacock's neck."[4] O'Connor's identification of Lucynell with the peacock immediately casts her in a special light—she is identified both with Christ and with one of the little ones Christ suffers to come unto him. Though she is not a child, in her affliction she looks and behaves like one. An innocent, totally absorbed by the wonder of the world she inhabits and completely taken with the new stranger, she is incapable of expressing her extraordinary vision. Shiftlet, on the other hand, uses language for insidious purposes, in this case to praise the sunset and moonrise falsely in order to get into Mrs. Crater's good graces, thereby disrespecting the sacredness of the creation and perverting the gift of language. In the course of the story, he will attempt to teach Lucynell to speak, but the only word she will master is "bird," a word suggesting key themes of the story, including flight, transcendence, and the presence of the Holy Spirit.

Shiftlet's burning desire for Mrs. Crater's car echoes another of O'Connor's characters, Hazel Motes, who also believes physical mobility releases the soul from its obligations towards God and the world. "Nobody with a good car needs to be justified," Hazel proclaims self-righteously as he claims his "high rat-colored car," which also will serve as the pulpit he preaches his nihilistic doctrines from.[5] Shiftlet's warped theology is gnostic in nature, separating the physical world from the divine: "The body, lady, is like a house: it don't go anywhere; but the spirit, lady, is like a automobile: always on the move, always. . . ."[6] Shiftlet eventually gets the car, but only in exchange for marrying Lucynell. Their wedding at the courthouse is a sham in his eyes, and he soon finds the opportunity he is looking for to dump her when he passes a roadside restaurant called "The Hot Spot." As he leaves Lucynell behind, slumped and snoring over the counter, exhausted from her big day, the boy waiting on them observes her long pink-gold hair and murmurs involuntarily, "She looks like an angel of Gawd."[7] In contrast to the boy's instinctive recognition, Shiftlet doesn't know holiness when he sees it. He abandons the sweet soul placed into his care and drives off towards Mobile (a destination whose name suggests his credo), ignoring the public service signs flanking the roadway bearing a warning message "The Life You Save May Be Your Own."[8]

Shiftlet bears all the marks of a sinner in full flight from his own redemption—the missing limb, the corrupt use of language, the use of a false identity (not only does it bear resemblance to the adjective "shifty," he telegraphs to Mrs. Crater that his name is invented). But the clearest sign of this resides in his anthem "The world is almost rotten," the signature sentence O'Connor chose as the original title for the story. (She changed the title to "The Life You Save May Be Your Own" at the suggestion of the Fitzgeralds, foregrounding Shiftlet's spiritual peril instead of his gnostic creed.) Like young John Wesley in "A Good Man Is Hard to Find" who wants to drive through Georgia fast so he won't have to look at it, Shiftlet sees no trace of the divine in creation. The world, for him, is not the Word of God made flesh—*fiat lux!*—miracle pervaded with mystery. Instead, it is merely a random collection of people for him to exploit and objects for him to possess. Shiftlet represents a type that shows up in O'Connor's fiction again and again—in the Misfit and Hazel Motes, among others—the restless soul who moves about the world enacting evil (whether consciously or not) and doing damage. O'Connor depicts such delusionists as mobile, in contrast to the stasis represented by characters such as Lucynell and her mother. For all of Mrs. Crater's faults, she is loyal to her farm, her place of birth, and the fruit of her labor. She, too, has taken a vow of place, which, if not monastic, serves the purpose of keeping her grounded in the real world and, potentially, the reality that lies behind it.

Here, again, it is not hard to see O'Connor's own predicament behind the story. Though she is primarily writing about the lives of others, she is simultaneously exploring the implications of her own grounded state, in search of the grace that her faith assures her comes with the (supposed) curses of life as well as its blessings.

"Good Country People"

Flannery's life at Andalusia was a round of regularity, the pattern of her days as deliberate and predictable as those of a consecrated monk. As Brad Gooch observes, "Flannery, dubbing herself a 'thirteenth century' Catholic at Yaddo and, at Andalusia, 'a hermit novelist,' framed her new life in religion."[9] Her day began very much as a monk's does, with Prime, or morning prayer, read from her breviary. After coffee, she and her mother drove into town to attend 7:00 a.m. Mass at their parish, Sacred Heart (always sitting in the same pew, the fifth on the right side). Upon their return, Flannery would spend several hours of inviolable time writing in her combination bedroom/studio while Regina busied herself with the running of the farm, driving around the twenty-one acre property, inspecting the barns and fields, and ensuring that work was being done. At noon, mother and daughter would abandon their labors and go to lunch at Sanford House, a tearoom located in the center of town and frequented by many of the local ladies (always occupying the same corner table). The mental clarity and energy that fueled Flannery's morning writing would dissipate by afternoon. She would then spend her hours engaging in her hobbies, including tending to her considerable herd of peacocks and oil painting, an activity she took up on return to Georgia, reviving her interest in the visual arts dating back to her childhood. On occasion, she and Regina would receive visitors—mostly friends and family, though as Flannery's fame grew, strangers would increasingly seek her out. After dinner, O'Connor would retire to her room, her day ending with sundown just as it had begun with sunrise. She would take up her breviary (located bedside beside her Bible and Sunday missal) and recite Compline, the last office of the day in the liturgy of hours (when she had the energy). Finally, she would read selections from the writings of St. Thomas Aquinas, her favorite theologian, from her Modern Library edition of his work.[10]

Though O'Connor enjoyed—and thrived on—this routine, the conditions of her life were less than ideal. A grown woman with a fiercely independent disposition, she'd been forced to return to live under her mother's roof, growing more and more dependent on her for her health and well-being each day. This situation would prove challenging to any daughter, but it was particularly difficult given how different the two women were. Regina was a practical woman, devoted to farm and family, and also a Southern lady, with all of the prejudices and provincialism that one associates with the term. Flannery, on the other hand, was an intellectual (despite her claims not to be), and a woman who had escaped the narrowness of her Southern upbringing by means of her education at Iowa and her northern sojourn. Regina would always be an insider in her culture (though her Catholicism set her somewhat apart from her Protestant neighbors). In contrast, Flannery would always be an outsider and an exile, situated *in* the rarified world of rural/small-town Georgia but not *of* it. Inevitably, mother and daughter did not see eye to eye, causing daily friction between them.

One might think this scenario a recipe for disastrous family life, but not so. As Flannery once quipped, "I come from a family where the only emotion respectable to show is irritation. In some this tendency produces hives, in others literature, in me both."[11] In fact, O'Connor's stories are full of mothers and daughters (as well as mothers, fathers, and sons) who do not get along. The sources of their difference vary greatly—as do the sources of difference from family to family—but the particular dynamic between an intelligent or educated daughter/son and a less enlightened mother, or a daughter/son who is dependent upon a parent ignorant of how to meet the child's needs—show up again and again in her stories, including "A Temple of the Holy Ghost," "The Life You Save May Be Your Own," "Everything That Rises Must Converge," "The River," "The Lame Shall Enter First," and "Revelation," among others. In some of these stories, the troubled parent-child nexus is minimal, a detail painted onto the canvas of the story in a brush stroke or two. The first story in which O'Connor depicts that relationship as central to the plot and to the inner life of the protagonist is "Good Country People," a story about a woman who owns a farm, her overly-educated daughter, and a Bible salesman who comes to their door one day.

"Nothing is perfect!" "That is life!" "Everybody is different!" "It takes all kinds to make the world!"[12] These are just a few of the many favorite expressions of Mrs. Hopewell, farm owner and mother to Joy Hopewell, a thirty-two-year-old with a weak heart, a wooden leg, and a PhD in philosophy. All three of these conditions pain her mother, but, having resigned herself to the first two years ago, the PhD seems to trouble her the most. "You could say, 'My daughter is a schoolteacher,' or even "My daughter is a chemical engineer.' You could not say, 'My daughter is a philosopher.' That was something that had ended with the Greeks and Romans."[13] In addition to her career choice, the relentlessly cheerful Mrs. Hopewell does not understand her daughter's melancholic disposition, her seething rage against the world, or her predilection for spending entire days immersed in reading books. One day, out of curiosity, her mother opens one of her books at random, comes upon a nihilistic passage about the nothingness of existence (sounding for all the world "like some evil incantation in gibberish") and slams it shut, frightened by the thoughts her daughter entertains. (O'Connor actually lifted the passage from her own copy of Heidegger's *Existence and Being*.) In response to one of her daughter's mystifying outbursts, during which she invokes the philosopher Malebranche to shed some light on her mother's dimness, Mrs. Hopewell's only response is to remind Joy that "a smile never hurt anyone."[14]

It is evident that Joy has done everything humanly possible to differentiate herself from her happy, hopeful, self-satisfied mother. This includes going away to school, choosing to lead the life of an intellectual, and, in an especially bold (and hurtful) gesture, changing her name from "Joy" to "Hulga," a name she selected mostly on the basis of its ugliness. She sees her renaming of herself—and redefining of her identity— "as her highest creative act," and congratulates herself at having succeeded in depriving her mother of the one of the satisfactions of parenthood: "One of her major triumphs was that her mother had not been able to turn her dust into Joy, but the greater one was that she had been able to turn it herself into Hulga."[15]

Though this is clearly a highly fictionalized, not to say exaggerated, version of the Regina-Flannery dynamic, it is not difficult to see O'Connor exploring the terrain of her own life. Instead of lupus, Hulga's heart condition has brought her back home and rendered her dependent; instead of a philosopher, Regina's daughter is a fiction writer; even the name change is a source of commonality between the two daughters, though O'Connor chose "Flannery" rather than "Hulga" to replace the first name her mother gave her. O'Connor recognized the kinship, however distant, between herself and her creation, confiding to Caroline Gordon and Alan Tate that Hulga represents what "I just by the grace of God escape being."[16]

The opening pages of O'Connor's story show mother and daughter locked in mortal combat. It will take some extraordinary event to break the deadlock they find themselves in, and that event takes the form of Manley Pointer's arrival. The young man, peddling his suitcase full of Bibles, appears to be simple and utterly innocent, a living, breathing manifestation of "good country people." This is one of the few things in the story Hulga and her mother agree upon. The hospitable Mrs. Hopewell invites him to stay for dinner—much to her reclusive daughter's disgust—and so begins Hulga's plan to seduce and humiliate the young man. Her motivation at first is pure meanness, the desire to demonstrate her superiority over both him and her mother, but as she goes forward with her plan, it becomes evident that Hulga is desperate for affection. Her plan backfires terribly: instead of the seduction and ruination of innocence she imagined perpetrating on Pointer, he fools her into giving up her most prized and private possession— her wooden leg—and abandons her in the hayloft on her mother's farm, stunned and humbled by her weakness and her folly in being duped by a fraud.

The conclusion of O'Connor's story is shocking. When he opens his suitcase, instead of being full of Bibles, it contains whiskey, prophylactics, and pornographic playing cards. To Hulga's horror, and in a moment of grotesque humor, it is into this valise that he places her beloved leg before he leaves. Virtually blind (he has removed her glasses) and left without a leg to stand on (actually and figuratively), Hulga's illusions about herself and the wooden crutch she leaned on for so long are removed. A supposed atheist, who prided herself on believing in nothing, she suddenly realizes that none of this has ever been true. Pointer is the true nihilist and faithful atheist, and he acts on those convictions rather than playing intellectual games. Hulga, too, is a fraud. Deep down, she is still Joy, her mother's daughter. O'Connor brings about this reversal swiftly and powerfully. As Paul Elie observes, "For all her learning, she is foolish; for all his simple ways, he is cunning. There are no good country people."[17]

Art & Life

Like the Misfit in "A Good Man Is Hard to Find," Manley Pointer is another of O'Connor's mysterious strangers who wreaks havoc in the lives of the characters who encounter him, opening the door to self-recognition and redemption. But in this particular story, like Hulga and Mrs. Hopewell, he also has a real-life counterpart. One late April afternoon in 1953, a young man arrived unexpectedly at Andalusia. Erik Langkjaer sold textbooks for Harcourt Brace, Flannery's publisher, and had been encouraged by local professors at her *alma mater* to visit O'Connor. Handsome, cosmopolitan, and well educated, Langkjaer had lived an itinerant life, having been born in Shanghai, lived in Copenhagen and New York City, and graduated from Princeton. Though he himself was not Catholic, he was urged by his cousin Helene Iswolsky, a Catholic intellectual and activist, to pursue graduate studies at Fordham University. After studying philosophy and teaching there for a brief time, his Jesuit mentor, William Lynch (one of O'Connor's favorite theologian/philosophers) suggested that, as a religious skeptic, he would not have a promising future at a Catholic college. For lack of a better plan, Langkjaer turned to publishing.

Flannery and Erik quickly discovered they had much in common. Both were intelligent, sophisticated and well read—qualities that marked them as outsiders in the community they were living in. Both felt a sense of homelessness, of not belonging to their respective worlds. Though Erik was not a believer, he was fascinated by theological questions and readily engaged in conversation with Flannery. Over the course of the next few months, he would return to Andalusia regularly—sometimes going as much as one hundred miles out of his way—for a total of ten or twelve visits, during which they would take long walks, go for car rides, or go out to lunch. O'Connor entered into a rare intimacy with Langkjaer. She discussed her disease—a deeply personal and private subject—in part to offer explanation for her swollen features and thinning hair, the results of the steroids she had to take. She also shared with him the painful fact of her father's premature death from lupus. Langkjaer, too, confided in Flannery, sharing an account of his troubled childhood in Denmark during the war and his father's death. When she gave Erik a copy of her book (he had not yet read *Wise Blood*), she inscribed it "For Erik who has wise blood too."[18]

Flannery's deep affection for Langkjaer is borne out in her letters written during this period, particularly those she addressed to him after he decided to return to Europe. The announcement of this decision in spring of 1954 troubled her deeply. Ostensibly, he was returning "home" to his native city to study at the University of Copenhagen, but he was also trying to put distance between himself and Flannery. Much as he admired her and enjoyed their friendship, he did not love her. Meanwhile, she carried her torch. In June of 1954, she writes, longingly, "I haven't seen any dirt roads since you left & I miss you."[19] In response to such letters, Erik sent the occasional postcard and, rarely, a brief note. Watching this transpire, Regina warned her daughter about the folly of carrying on a lopsided correspondence, and so the letters grew fewer and further between.

In February of 1955, Flannery wrote "Good Country People," full of its "coded references" to Erik, particularly in Manley's job as a fake Bible salesman, his vague origins and itinerant life, and his sudden exit after extracting from Hulga her deepest secrets.[20] It took O'Connor only four days, the fastest piece she ever wrote. Two months later, Flannery received a note announcing Erik's engagement to a woman he had fallen in love with in Denmark—he would be married in July. For the next three years O'Connor continued her correspondence with him, but with a difference. The letters were friendly but formal, brief and polite. She would never see him again. Years later, when Sally Fitzgerald asked Regina whether Flannery had suffered over the breakup, Regina looked down before replying, "Yes, she did, it was terrible."[21]

Though O'Connor experienced desolation at the loss of Erik, she must have been consoled by her achievements in terms of her work as a writer. On June 6, 1955, her first collection, *A Good Man Is Hard to Find and Other Stories,* was published to great critical acclaim. In addition, she signed a contract with Harcourt Brace for her new novel; she won a second O. Henry prize for "The Life You Save May Be Your Own"; a number of her stories, including "Good Country People," were appearing in fine journals; and *Wise Blood* was published in England, making her work available to a whole new audience of readers. In short, her career was taking off.

The experience with Langkjaer was, in fact, instructive. Just as Hulga Hopewell sees herself and her life through new eyes with the departure of her would-be lover, Flannery must have come to a fuller understanding of her own situation. Though she had taken no vows of celibacy, she was almost certainly going to be confined to living a celibate life. Marooned as she was, she would not find love in the larger world, and there was little likelihood of another Erik

Langkjaer showing up (for better or for worse). Thus, after this brief interlude, life at Andalusia returned to its regular round, with Flannery newly resigned to her exile, reconfirmed in her vow of stability, and recommitted to her vocation: cherishing the world as she struggled to endure it.

CHAPTER SIX

Faith & Art (1956–59)

The Journey to the Province of Joy

"A couple of years ago the Catholic Worker sent
me a card on which was printed a prayer to St.
Raphael. . . . The prayer asks St. Raphael to guide
us to the province of joy so that we may not be
ignorant of the concerns of our true country."[1]
—Letter to Betty Hester, 1956

In spite of the fact of O'Connor's geographical fixity, she
always understood herself to be on pilgrimage. Late in 1955,
she learned that the gradual degeneration of her hipbones
had progressed and that she would need to use crutches for
a year or two. Referring to them as her "flying buttresses,"
O'Connor received this news with her characteristic stoicism
and good humor, even as her condition worsened in the
following year and she learned the crutches would be permanent.[2] Though her physical movement became more re-
stricted, the pace of her intellectual and spiritual journey
never slowed or slackened. As a writer and a Catholic,

O'Connor advanced along the journey through the twin practices of her faith and her art, and she never lost sight of her destination.

The prayer to St. Raphael cited in the epigraph was one O'Connor said every morning for many years as part of her daily office; she found both freedom and consolation in this prayer. In the face of loneliness, isolation, constant physical pain and limitation, and the psychological burden of living with a fatal disease, her daily appeal to St. Raphael, "the Angel of Happy Meeting," was a daily passage to "the province of joy." O'Connor knew that the "true country," the proper destination, orientation, and disposition of a believing Christian, is joy—a word with a rich history of theological nuance, suggesting as it does both heaven (a place towards which we tend) and paradise (the place where human beings originated). In both cases, joy is a place and circumstance that belongs to us. Through prayer and through her writing, which served as a kind of prayer for O'Connor, she could place herself on the threshold of that province using the power of the word and the imagination.

Prayer was a means of movement for O'Connor. It could propel her from the limited place in which she found herself toward the limitless space of joy, a location that can be occupied in the here and now, as well as looked forward to in eternity. In George Herbert's celebration of prayer, he describes the place it takes one to as "the land of spices."[3] Another praying poet, Emily Dickinson, describes the paradox of prayer emphasizing its locomotive power: "Instead of getting to heaven at last/I'm going all along."[4] Both poets, along with O'Connor, know that prayer transports the pray-er through the here-and-now, providing her with a foretaste of paradise.[5]

There is little wonder that O'Connor felt compelled to share this prayer with her most intimate friends. Nine years after the letter quoted in the epigraph, on July 14, 1964, just three weeks before her death, Flannery enclosed the prayer in a letter to another friend. It is moving to imagine O'Connor, never to rise again from her sickbed, laboriously copying out these words that had meant so much to her as a final farewell gift.

> O Raphael, lead us toward those we are waiting for, those who are waiting for us: Raphael, Angel of happy meeting, lead us by the hand toward those we are looking for. May all our movements be guided by your Light and transfigured with your joy.
>
> Angel, guide of Tobias, lay the request we now address to you at the feet of Him on whose unveiled Face you are privileged to gaze. Lonely and tired, crushed by the separations and sorrows of life, we feel the need of calling you and of pleading for the protection of your wings, so that we may not be as strangers in the province of joy, all ignorant of the concerns of our country. Remember the weak, you who are strong, you whose home lies beyond the region of thunder, in a land that is always peaceful, always serene and bright with the resplendent glory of God.[6]

An Epistolary Ministry

O'Connor had long been devoted to the discipline of letter writing. One needs only to recall her daily letters to her mother during the years she lived away from Georgia to understand the degree to which she depended on written correspondence as a means of maintaining intimacy with absent people she loved. As O'Connor's fame as a writer grew, her circle of correspondents grew as well. She would frequently receive letters from admirers and critics of her stories—some of whom were "freakish," in the words of Paul

Elie, including "several patients in insane asylums, a truck driver who insisted that a good man really wasn't so hard to find, and a woman who read 'A Temple of the Holy Ghost' as a lesbian allegory."[7] "I seem to attract the lunatic fringe," O'Connor once quipped.[8] O'Connor would faithfully respond to these letters, often out of a sense of duty, but in the course of her career, she would enter into some remarkable correspondences with a range of remarkable people, resulting in relationships that would continue for years and effectively carrying on conversations that would shape the lives of all involved. In *The Habit of Being*, the selection of O'Connor's letters Sally Fitzgerald collected and edited after her death, readers can eavesdrop on these conversations—at least, Flannery's side of them—and vicariously experience them. Not surprisingly, the focus is as often on faith as it is on fiction. These letters, in particular, were not only labors of love; they demonstrate O'Connor's extraordinary capacity for theological inquiry and elevate O'Connor's epistolary practice from a discipline to the level of art.

One such correspondence was between O'Connor and Betty Hester, a credit company clerk in Atlanta who wrote a fan letter to Flannery in July of 1955, thereby initiating a nine-year epistolary conversation that would end only with O'Connor's death. On July 20, Flannery responded to Hester's letter with enthusiasm, as the young woman had divined the truth at the root of O'Connor's fiction—her stories were about God: "I am very pleased to have your letter. Perhaps it is even more startling to me to find someone who recognizes my work for what I try to make it than it is for you to find a God-conscious writer near at hand. The distance is eighty-seven miles but I feel the spiritual distance is shorter."[9] On this note of kinship begins a relationship in which Flannery will serve as Betty's friend, philosopher, and guide—acting at times as her spiritual director—and enabling O'Connor to write, in the course of her 150 letters to Hester, freely and openly about her faith and its relationship to her art. As biographer Jonathan Rogers asserts, "The story of Flannery O'Connor's life is the story of her inner life more than her outer life. The Betty Hester letters, like nothing else in the body of O'Connor's work, shed light on that inner life—who she was as a believer, as a writer, as a Southerner, as a human being."[10] In her first letter to Hester, she writes about her Catholicism with directness and candor:

> I write the way I do because (not though) I am a Catholic. This is a fact and nothing covers it like the bald statement. However, I am a Catholic peculiarly possessed of the modern consciousness, the thing Jung describes as unhistorical, solitary, and guilty. To possess this within the church is to bear a burden, the necessary burden for the conscious Catholic. It's to feel the contemporary situation at the ultimate level. I think that the Church is the only thing that is going to make the terrible world we are coming to endurable; the only thing that makes the Church endurable is that it is somehow the body of Christ and on that we are fed. It seems to be a fact that you have to suffer as much from the Church as for it. . . ."[11]

O'Connor captures deftly here the conflict inherent in being a believer in a culture of unbelief, and particularly the struggle of being a Catholic in a world wherein no one believes in enchantment, in the presence of the supernatural in the natural. The church, for Flannery, is the only source of salvation in an increasingly troubled world. (We scarcely need to recall the historical context of her observations, written just a few years after the end of World War II, the unveiling of the horrors of Holocaust, the destruction of Hiroshima and Nagasaki, the introduction of nuclear weapons into the world's arsenal, and the heating up of the Cold War.) Yet it is not exactly a safe harbor. In words that sound like they might have been written yesterday, O'Connor acknowledges the flaws and the scandal of the church. As a human institution, it is far from perfect, and human beings suffer at its hands as surely as they suffer from other imperfect institutions. Yet it is somehow in that human suffering that one finds Christ, the one who both endures and redeems it.

O'Connor's witness to her Catholicism would make a deep impression on Hester. Never trying consciously to convert her friend or to idealize her religion, Flannery is as honest with Hester about her doubts as she is about her faith: "When I ask myself how I know I believe, I have no satisfactory answer at all, no assurance at all, no feeling at all. I can only say with Peter, Lord I believe, help my unbelief. And all I can say about my love of God is, Lord help me in my lack of it. I distrust pious phrases, particularly when they issue from my mouth."[12] Such lessons in spiritual humility were not lost on Hester. In addition, Flannery inadvertently served as catechist for Betty. The two women would correspond about a host of Catholic and religious writers, including Dante, St. Augustine, St. Thomas Aquinas, St. Catherine of Siena, Romano Guardini, Etienne Gilson, Simone Weil, and William Lynch, to name but a few, and converse about fine points of church teaching. Yet despite all of this heady religious dialogue, O'Connor was surprised to learn in January 1956 that Hester wished to become a Catholic convert: "I'm never prepared for anything . . . I have been equally positive that you were a Pantheist in good standing . . . and now you're as orthodox as I am if not more."[13] From here on out, a new tonality enters into the letters the women share—that of intimacy. As Paul Elie remarks, "the Other, the opposite, became a conspirator, a fellow member of the Mystical Body of Christ."[14] When Hester is baptized and confirmed at Eastertime in Atlanta, O'Connor would send her a breviary, like her own (given to her by the Fitzgeralds), she would attend Mass at her parish in Milledgeville with Betty in mind, and she would receive Communion for her. She writes to her friend, "since we will then share the same actual food, you will know that your being where you are increases me and the other way around."[15]

In addition to their important religious dimension, Paul Elie remarks that the correspondence between O'Connor and Hester "dominates *The Habit of Being*, and it has shaped the interpretations of O'Connor's fiction more than anything else she wrote. This is just as she wanted it."[16] Writing to Betty gave Flannery the occasion to clarify her literary doctrines, grounding them in the spiritual ones she subscribed to. Betty served as a sounding board for her as Flannery worked them out in her own mind. Moreover, O'Connor was aware that these letters would likely be available for posterity, so in a sense, she is not only writing for Betty Hester; she is writing for us. This effect is further increased by the fact that Sally Fitzgerald, in editing the letters, refers to Hester only as "A," in effort to protect her privacy. Until recently, when Hester's identity was revealed, the reader of O'Connor's letters could entertain the notion that the nameless, faceless, identity-less "A" O'Connor addresses could very well be he. Regardless of for whom they were intended, our understanding of O'Connor as a consciously Catholic writer owes much to this rich exchange between these two women.

O'Connor corresponded with a number of other people who would prove important in her life. Among these is William Sessions, a young writer and teacher she met in July of 1956, with whom she began a long correspondence—much of it taken up with matters of art and faith—and a lifelong friendship. In that same year, Flannery would make the acquaintance of James McCown, a Jesuit priest who traveled to Andalusia in order to share his admiration for her work. McCown would become a trusted friend and advisor to O'Connor, as well as a promoter of her work in Catholic circles. At his recommendation, she would begin to write for *America*, the Jesuit weekly magazine, giving her further opportunity to articulate the complex relationship between her Catholicism and her vocation as a fiction writer. O'Connor's celebrated essay, "The Church and the Fiction Writer" would appear the following year, on March 30, 1957, in the pages of the journal, making her ideas about faith and writing widely available to a specifically Catholic readership. During this period, she would also write multiple book reviews for the Atlanta diocesan weekly, *The Bulletin*, thereby helping to shape the taste by which literary and theological works would be evaluated by a Catholic audience. Through 1964, O'Connor would publish 120 reviews, mostly for Georgia diocesan papers—work she considered to be a form of service to the church. Finally, in late December of 1956, O'Connor would meet playwright Maryat Lee, sister of the president of her alma mater (Georgia State College for Women), who lived in New York. Urbane and charismatic, a fellow artist who had forsaken the South to live in the city of aspiring artists, Maryat was a very different kind of friend and correspondent. Writing to her as an equal, O'Connor could be playful, funny, irreverent, and blunt about matters that interested them, especially literary ones. In addition, as a former Southerner who had adopted Northern values, Maryat would put Flannery's ideas about social codes, including her attitudes towards race (always a vexed subject for the Southern writer) to the test.

Even as O'Connor was expanding her social network, she was also getting out into the world, despite her physical limitations. During 1956–57, Flannery would give lectures for the Lansing, Michigan, chapter of the American Association of University Women; at Emory University (among other Southern colleges); at the University of Notre Dame in South Bend, Indiana; and at numerous local club and literary meetings. These appearances gave her the opportunity to earn speakers' fees and also to engage in direct conversation with her readers.

Her most ambitious journey, however, was the seventeen-day pilgrimage she and Regina made to Lourdes in April and May of 1958. O'Connor had misgivings about the trip and the questionable theology behind the miracle cures pious Catholics associated with Lourdes, but Flannery's cousin Katie Semmes of Savannah insisted that she avail herself of every opportunity to get well and would provide the funds. Bested by family loyalty, and perhaps a sense of curiosity as well, on the Thursday after Easter, a century after the Virgin Mary appeared to young Bernadette Soubirous, Flannery and Regina made their way to Europe, stopping first in Milan, then in Levanto to visit the Fitzgeralds (who had been living there for some years having taken a sabbatical from their lives in Connecticut), then traveling to Paris by train, and then to the village of Lourdes in the Pyrenees.[17] O'Connor had mocked the idea of the pilgrimage in her letters to Betty Hester, referring to it as a "comic nightmare," dreading being one of a "planeload of fortress-footed female Catholics pushed from shrine to shrine," but her letters afterward suggest that she was glad to have made the journey: "Lourdes was not as bad as I expected it to be."[18] Despite her resolve not to bathe in or drink the healing waters, she did both (evidently in response to Sally

Fitzgerald's warning that she not turn away from grace). Typical of Flannery, though, she claims to have prayed more for her book than her bones.[19] At the time, O'Connor was still struggling mightily with her second novel, and one of the effects of her pilgrimage (and her time away from the book) was that she returned to work on it with renewed vigor. By January of 1959, just eight months after her return to the United States, she completed a first draft of the book, now titled *The Violent Bear It Away*. Another possible effect, however, was the unexpected news in November that x-rays showed her bones to be improving, so much so she was able to walk around the house without her crutches. O'Connor was willing to grant that the pilgrimage to Lourdes may have been responsible for this healing and was able to share the hopeful news with her cousin Katie Semmes shortly before her death.

Upon returning to Andalusia, O'Connor wrote to Sally and Robert Fitzgerald, thanking them for their hospitality in Italy, clearly grateful for the chance to see her old friends, but also grateful to be back in Georgia: "As for me, my capacity for staying at home has been greatly increased. It is doubtful if after this trip to Missouri I will ever depart from Baldwin County again."[20] O'Connor had grown accustomed to living in her place of supposed exile. Perhaps this is because she had discovered the fact that she didn't need to engage in physical travel in order to be on pilgrimage. Given the powerful modes of communication and communion given to her—via prayer, her writing and reviewing, and letters exchanged with admiring fans and beloved friends—O'Connor had come to realize that any locale she inhabited had the potential to become the province of joy, the place toward which she was both tending and that she already occupied.

CHAPTER SEVEN

Saints, Sinners, Race & Grace
(1960–62)

"Even the Mercy of the Lord Burns"

> "What people don't realize is how much religion costs. They think faith is a big electric blanket, when of course it is the cross."[1]
> —Letter to Louise Abbot, 1959

On February 8, 1960, O'Connor's second novel, *The Violent Bear It Away,* was published. She had labored over the book for seven years—two years longer than on *Wise Blood*—and when she finished it, she felt its flaws: "I have the galley proofs of my novel and have been correcting them and it is very depressing to see the thing in print. It is dull and half-done and I will not be able to blame anybody for not liking it. I can barely force myself along."[2] This painfully honest admission Flannery makes to Betty Hester reflects a perfectionist's typical dissatisfaction with her work (she had similarly written that reading the proofs of *Wise Blood* was like "eating a horse blanket"[3]), but it also reflects her concern that readers will misunderstand the book. Just a few weeks earlier, she had written with confidence to another correspondent, John Hawkes, summarizing the book's import: "I don't think you should write something as long as a novel around anything that is not of the greatest concern to you and everybody else and for me this is always the conflict between an attraction for the Holy and the disbelief in it that we breathe in with the air of the times. It's hard to believe always but more so in the world we live in now."[4]

The Violent Bear It Away dramatizes precisely this conflict between contemporary rationalism and the urgent call to belief, represented by the characters of Old Francis Marion Tarwater, a Southern backwoods prophet, and Rayber, nicknamed "schoolteacher" for his belief in the intellect, rather than the spirit, as a trustworthy guide to truth. At the center of their conflict is a young boy, also called Tarwater, great-nephew to the old man, over whose soul the two men battle. The novel opens with the death of the old man, and young Tarwater has to decide which calling to choose—the role of prophet he has been brought up to or the role of nonbelieving secular humanist modeled by his schoolteacher uncle. O'Connor seems to know precisely how her novel is likely to be misread: "The modern reader will identify himself with the schoolteacher, but it is the old man who speaks for me."[5] As it turned out, O'Connor was right—both she and "the old man" were misunderstood. Critics saw Tarwater as another "God-intoxicated hillbilly" O'Connor seemed to be satirizing, whereas, in reality, she was attempting to depict the errant but genuine ways in which human beings fumble blindly toward the grace they instinctively know is available to them.[6] Like Hazel Motes, old Tarwater is both guided and misguided by a deep hunger for Jesus, the bread of life, driven by his wise blood. The force of his relentless faith terrifies his great-nephew: "The boy sensed that this was the heart of his great-uncle's madness, this hunger, and what he was secretly afraid of was that it might be passed down, might be hidden in the blood and might strike some day in him and then he would be torn by hunger like the old man, the bottom split out of his stomach so that nothing would heal or fill it but the bread of life."[7] When the old man dies unexpectedly at the beginning of the novel, Tarwater tries to escape his own wise blood and his destiny by running away to the city to find the uncle that old Tarwater so despised. Instead of a trustworthy adult, he finds, in Rayber, a man trying to convince himself of ideas he knows are not true. Like other O'Connor characters who are neither sound nor whole, Rayber suffers from a physical limitation that is emblematic of a spiritual one—profoundly deaf, he cannot hear the word of God. He also possesses a mentally handicapped son he alternately adores and despises; reason can't account for any purpose to his child's existence, nor can it account for Rayber's own instinctive love. Tragedy ensues, as young Tarwater pursues his late great-uncle's fixation on baptizing the child—a sacramental practice that goes terribly wrong—and Tarwater heads home in effort to make peace with his past and the old man's ghost. But even in this he is thwarted, as the young man encounters evil along the journey, suffering physical violation at the hands of a wandering pederast, and finds himself working out his salvation in fear and trembling.

Both in literary and theological terms, all of this is vintage O'Connor. The events that befall young Tarwater—even the most violent and horrific—are all necessary to his conversion. Like the grandmother in "A Good Man Is Hard to Find," who must see her family murdered before she truly understands the nature of good and evil, Tarwater must bear witness to evil before he can choose the good. In one of her essays (quoted earlier in chapter 2), O'Connor notes, "I have found that violence is strangely capable of returning my characters to reality and preparing them to accept their moment of grace. Their heads are so hard that almost nothing else will do the work."[8] Such actions are all part of the fierce economy of grace that characterizes O'Connor's vision. She had little patience with soft views of Christianity in which the challenge of Christ's message and example is blunted and bowdlerized to make it palatable to modern sensibilities: "This notion that grace is healing omits the fact that before it heals, it cuts with the sword Christ said he came to bring."[9] Hers is a vision of a sacramental universe in which all of nature participates in the divine plan—even serial killers and pederasts. Frequently, the action that precipitates conversion in one of her characters "is an action in which the devil has been the unwilling instrument of grace."[10] All things are possible with God, and that includes bringing good out of evil.

Slavery, Segregation & Racism: The Sins of the South

Dark as the vision of her novel—and of the human sinner—may seem, *The Violent Bear It Away* is not devoid of virtuous characters. Buford, the man we meet at the beginning and end of the novel, performs the single, central moral act in the story in burying the body of old Tarwater and placing a cross on the grave. When the old man dies, his great-nephew finds himself unable to dig the grave, so he abandons the corpse and retires to the family still to get drunk. Buford takes up the burden, unbeknown to young Tarwater, and finally reveals his work of corporal mercy to him at the end of the novel when the boy returns: "It's owing to me he's resting there. I buried him while you were laid out drunk. It's owing to me his corn has been plowed. It's owing to me the sign of his Saviour is over his head."[11] Buford's identity as a vessel of saving grace is signaled in Tarwater's first sighting of him as he approaches the boy: "Then near the stall he saw a Negro mounted on a mule. The mule was not moving: the two might have been made out of rock."[12] The iconographic association of Buford with Christ comes through clearly, in both his position astride a donkey (like Christ on Palm Sunday) and in is his steadfast, rocklike presence in Tarwater's life, despite all of the latter's wayward wanderings. Only slowly does the boy recognize this powerful presence as that of Buford. Perhaps the most remarkable thing about this passage is the fact that the one good man (who is always hard to find) in this world of decadent white men is a black man.

Writing in the early civil rights-era, racist South, O'Connor makes a profound statement in making Tarwater's savior African American. Slavery is the dreadful, unspoken sin of the South in O'Connor's fiction; it casts a looming presence, more palpable for the silence surrounding it. Though depiction of that historical institution may be absent, however, what is often painfully present is the legacy of slavery in the form of deep-seated, and often unconscious, racism. At times, this comes through subtly and is reflected mostly in the condescending attitudes of white characters towards blacks. At other times, it is less subtle and is most vividly present and troubling in O'Connor's use of language, particularly in the liberal use of the word *nigger* to describe black characters. On the one hand, the use of the word is very much in keeping with a realistic depiction of the world O'Connor's stories are set in; she is writing about a region that is afflicted with the sin of racism, and this is how racist people talk. What is at issue for readers of O'Connor is the degree to which she participated in that culture. Are her characters simply mouthpieces, reflecting inappropriate racial attitudes? Or do they also, in some way, speak for her? On the one hand, the characterization of Buford—along with the use of the respectful term *negro* instead of its crass counterpart—suggests an enlightened vision, one that casts the Southern black man in the role of righteous, responsible Christian soul, an oasis of sanity in a parched world. However, this sort of respect is undercut by attitudes toward African Americans O'Connor expresses in some of her very early stories and, most disturbingly, in her letters.

Biographer Paul Elie notes this contradiction in O'Connor's writings: "Where did Flannery O'Connor stand in matters of race? The evidence tells two ways. Black characters in O'Connor's fiction are invariably admirable. . . . Yet at the same time there is the word "nigger" running through the correspondence. There is, in the letters, a habit of bigotry that grows more pronounced as O'Connor's fiction, in matters of race, grows more complex and profound—a habit that seems to defy the pattern established by her art."[13]

Elie here acknowledges the progress O'Connor makes in the depiction of black characters in her fiction in the course of her career. One explanation for that progress lies, perhaps, in her education. It is not surprising that a child growing up in the South before the civil rights era would adopt the racial attitudes passed down to her by her parents and held by the community and larger culture she is a part of. Thus, when Flannery went off to Iowa, she carried the prejudices of her region with her. On one occasion, when visiting writer (and fellow Southerner) John Crowe Ransom came to visit her classroom, he chose one of O'Connor's stories to read to the class; however, when he came across the word *nigger*, he refused to read it and substituted, instead, the more benign word *negro*. O'Connor was troubled and mystified: "It did spoil the story," she complained to one of her Iowa instructors. "The people I was writing about would never use any other word."[14] Young Flannery's misunderstanding here is instructive: Ransom had seen more of the world and understood how fraught that term was, even if it was being used for the purposes of accurately capturing the dialogue of poor Southern whites. The word, with its power to wound and violate, did not translate outside of the context of the South, and so he chose to omit it. Gradually, after moving north and living in New York and Connecticut, Flannery, too, would observe the ways in which the customs of that country differed from those of her own. It would further sensitize her to the use of the word in her stories. Though, in the interest of verisimilitude, she could not strike it from the vocabulary of her fiction, it is used almost exclusively by her characters, either in dialogue with others or in interior monologues, but not by the narrator. The term reflects *their* racism—and all of the suggestions of provincialism, narrow-mindedness, and sin that go with it—not hers.

The letters, however, tell another story. Finding herself living in the South again, O'Connor seemed to adapt, once more, to the customs of that world. In one particularly telling incident, her friend and correspondent Maryat Lee asked O'Connor if she might be willing to have African-American writer James Baldwin visit her home. Flannery's response is unequivocal: "No I can't see James Baldwin in Georgia. It would cause the greatest trouble and disturbance and disunion. In New York it would be nice to meet him: here it would not. I observe the traditions of the society I feed on—it's only fair. Might as well expect a mule to fly as me to see James Baldwin in Georgia. I have read one of his stories and it was a good one."[15]

The letter itself embodies O'Connor's contradictory attitude: both her admiration of Baldwin as a writer and her inability to meet with him as a colleague and an equal. The key to her response, though, lies in the different manners and expectations associated with the two very different worlds she has lived in—New York and Georgia. In April of 1959 (the date of the letter), rural Georgia was a place untouched (as yet) by racial unrest. Free blacks and whites had been living together for a century, yet they might as well have lived worlds apart, obeying a careful code of "separate but equal." These established norms were kept in force through a rigid system of apartheid (Jim Crow laws) and through the very real threat of violence from the Ku Klux Klan. In another telling incident, O'Connor describes in a letter to Maryat Lee the events that occurred on the campus of her alma mater in the late 1940s wherein two negro teachers attended an education conference held at the university: "The story goes that everything was as separate and equal as possible, even down to two Coca-Cola machines, white and colored; but that night a cross was burned on Dr. Wells' [the college president's] side lawn. And those times weren't as troubled as these. The people who burned the cross couldn't have gone past the fourth grade but, for the time they were mighty interested in education."[16] Much of the South, both white and black (as well as Catholic and Jew), lived in thrall to a terrorist organization that made sure there was no contact between blacks and whites that they judged to be illicit. Given this, it is no wonder O'Connor could not host Baldwin at her home. To do so would scandalize her neighbors, offend her mother, and put them all in almost certain danger. Seen in this context, her decision to abide by "the traditions of the society she feeds on" seems more a survival mechanism than an endorsement of racial intolerance.

Nonetheless, the contradiction stands, some of which might be accounted for with the aid of historical contextualization. In many of her letters with Maryat Lee during the era of the civil rights movement, O'Connor reveals her "habit of bigotry," often doing so, it seems, to critique the liberal politics of her liberal white friend. While most of the nation (especially those in the North) was witnessing what would be historic events from a distance—the bus boycott on Montgomery, Alabama, led by Martin Luther King in 1955; the integration of Central High School in Little Rock, Arkansas, in 1957; and the first sit-in at a Woolworth's lunch counter in Greensboro, North Carolina, in 1960—Southerners felt these as seismic waves that threatened to bring their world crashing down around them. This brought about a sense of fear, uncertainty, and profound ambivalence, even in white Southerners who were sympathetic to the plight of African Americans. It was especially troubling to them to see white Northerners coming into the South, bringing with them a sense of Yankee superiority and interfering with the handling of their racial problems. In the context of these events, Maryat and Flannery developed a kind of patter in their correspondence, described by biographer Brad Gooch: "Maryat was cast as the ultimate Northern liberal, and Flannery a bigoted Southern redneck. Unfortunately, in a number of these letters, many still unpublished, Flannery slipped into her role too easily, her mask fitting disconcertingly well. She turned out to be a connoisseur of racial jokes, regaling Maryat with offensive punch lines."[17] The two women adopted pet names as part of this game, and, along with them, alternate personalities: Flannery dubbed Maryat as Raybutter, Raybalm, and Rayfish—all variations on Ray-ber, Maryat's favorite character in *The Violent Bear It Away*—and Maryat invented nicknames for Flannery based on the boy prophet she so identified with, including Tarbabe, Tarsoul, Tarsquawk, and Tarfunk. It is impossible to know the degree to which O'Connor's participation in this play was ironic, her jokes told purely for effect in a lame (not to mention insensitive) attempt at humor, and the degree to which she actually believed in the racial inferiority these jokes assumed. Much as we might like to know the heart of any writer—or any human being for that matter—the full mystery of the human personality cannot be fathomed.

This is not to excuse O'Connor's racial attitudes. If, by some miraculous suspension of the laws of time and space, we were able to interrogate her on the charge of racism, it's reasonable to believe that she would own up to it. O'Connor never claimed to be unafflicted by sin—quite the contrary, it was through her knowledge of her own sin that she was able to see the sins of her characters so clearly: "I am not a mystic and I do not lead a holy life. Not that I can claim any interesting or pleasurable sins (my sense of the devil is strong) but I know all about the garden variety, pride, glut-tony, envy and sloth, and what is more to the point, my virtues are as timid as my vices. I think sin occasionally brings one closer to God. . . . A working knowledge of the devil can be very well had from resisting him."[18]

No writer is paragon of moral virtue, even those who are most vigilant—and yet, so many artists who were deeply flawed people have managed to create powerful art that transcends their personal limitations. Given this, perhaps the wisest course of action in assessing O'Connor's—and any writer's—contribution to literary posterity is to focus on the work rather than the life, and, to paraphrase the famous words of D. H. Lawrence, to trust the tale rather than the teller.

Theology & Race: Teilhard de Chardin & "Everything That Rises Must Converge"

If education played a key role in O'Connor's gradual sensitization to the plight of African Americans in her stories, a key moment in that process was the discovery of the writings of the French Jesuit priest and philosopher Teilhard de Chardin. O'Connor first heard of his books from her publisher, Robert Giroux, in May of 1959, and thus began a fascination with his work that would inform both her theological vision and her fiction. After his death in 1955, Teilhard's works were being translated into English. Available to her for the first time, O'Connor was quick to read them as they were published and to review them for Catholic magazines in her enthusiasm to share them with readers. Part paleontologist, part philosopher, part poet, and part theologian, Teilhard created in his books a vision that brought all of these seemingly disparate pursuits of the intellect and the imagination into sync. In *The Divine Milieu,* O'Connor's favorite book by her new spiritual master, Teilhard offered a narrative depicting a world that was gradually evolving into being, slowly moving towards its ultimate transformation or divinization. Matter and spirit worked together, in his prophetic vision, the incarnation a single ongoing event that would inexorably shape the physical world—and everyone in it—into the Mystical Body of Christ. Teilhard's endorsement of evolution and his belief in the sentience of matter made him unpopular with the church and among his fellow scientists. The Vatican had banned his works from Catholic bookstores in 1957—a fact that troubled O'Connor—but she remained convinced that Teilhard would be vindicated—canonized, in fact—and that his writings would eventually be appreciated for the brilliant and blessed truth they offered.

In March of 1961, O'Connor wrote her only truly topical story, one that focused directly on the issue of race: "Everything That Rises Must Converge." The title is a direct quotation of one of Teilhard's essays, thus signaling her debt to this new vision of the evolving unity, or convergence, she had been given a glimpse of. O'Connor explains her intentions quite clearly in a letter to Roslyn Barnes, a young Catholic writer studying at Iowa: the term is "a physical proposition that I found in Pere Teilhard and am applying to a certain situation in the Southern states and indeed in all the world."[19] The primary setting of the story is a city bus—a common mode of transportation that sparked the civil rights movement and became a battleground between blacks and whites. The protagonists are a mother and son—each representing a different generation and a different attitude towards the South and towards African Americans. Julian is an educated young man with progressive ideas who is forced by circumstance to live at home. Barely able to tolerate his mother's racism, her pride in her patrician past, and her nostalgia for the days of slavery when blacks and whites knew their respective places in society, he suffers a martyr complex, seeing himself as a modern day Saint Sebastian pierced daily by the arrows his mother aims at him.

Julian, however, is no saint. Though his mother is guilty of racial sin, she is totally devoted to her only child. Having raised him alone and made sacrifices so that he might receive an education (the very education that has sown division between them), and blinded by love for him, he is her sole source of pride and joy. For all her flaws, she is a good mother. He, on the other hand, is not a good son. His pleasure in challenging his mother's outmoded ideas crosses the boundary from self-righteous rhetoric into a mild form of sadism one evening when they board the bus en route to her exercise class in the city. Following an evil urge to "break her spirit" and teach her a lesson, Julian seats himself next to a black man and attempts to make conversation, all the while fantasizing about making friends with black people and bringing home a black woman as his fiancée. Thwarted in his attempt at camaraderie by the black man, who wisely wants no part of conversation with Julian, he finds an even better vehicle for his mother's humiliation when a large black woman boards the bus with her little boy. The woman is wearing a hideous green and purple hat that is identical to the one his mother is wearing. From this point on, Julian does everything he can to drive home to his mother the apparent equality between the two women, suggested by the similarity of their headwear, and her own absurdity.

Julian's goading of his mother—along with her own foolish observance of the custom of *noblesse oblige* towards the woman's child in the form of giving him a penny—eventually leads to violent confrontation between the two mothers, and the story ends in tragedy. Julian becomes poignantly aware, as he watches his mother suffer a fatal stroke, that he has been the true instrument of her death. Suddenly all of his supposedly high-minded thinking about racial equality evaporates, being the pure abstraction that it was. In choosing the idol of an idea over the physical embodiment of love his mother represented, Julian (like so many of O'Connor's errant characters) was living in his head and not in the real world. Though the story doesn't offer any solutions for the South's racial divisions—apart from the assurance implied by the title that convergence of the races (as well as of the generations, of mothers and sons, and of all other apparent contraries) will occur in the fullness of time as part of the divine plan—it clearly demonstrates that one can't heal the sins of slavery, segregation, and racism by sacrificing one's mother on the altar of social progress. Julian feels the full brunt of his own brutality as he watches her lurch away from him: "A tide of darkness seemed to be sweeping her from him. 'Mother!' he cried. 'Darling, sweetheart, wait!' " But she can't wait, and she won't. Julian is left poised on the brink of a new dispensation, though he is reluctant to enter the new life he has inherited, "postponing from moment to moment his entry into the world of guilt and sorrow."[20]

O'Connor leaves Julian, much as she leaves young Tarwater, on the threshold of discovery of a new country. Guilt and sorrow are not desirable states for human beings to occupy—we resist them with all of our being. Yet they are the conduits of grace, the means through which sinners experience the mercy of God. As old Tarwater teaches his young nephew, as Julian discovers, and as O'Connor herself learned in suffering the affliction of her illness and her sense of her own sin—in matters racial and otherwise—the lessons human beings learn are hard. Indeed, "even the mercy of the Lord burns."[21]

CHAPTER EIGHT

Revelations & Last Acts
(1963–64)

Facing the Dragon

"St. Cyril of Jerusalem, in instructing catechumens, wrote: 'The dragon sits by the side of the road, watching those who pass. Beware lest he devour you. We go to the Father of Souls, but it is necessary to pass by the dragon.' No matter what form the dragon may take, it is of this mysterious passage past him, or into his jaws, that stories of any depth will always be concerned to tell, and this being the case, it requires considerable courage at any time, in any country, not to turn away from the storyteller."[1]

—*Mystery and Manners*

O'Connor reports her initial discovery of this passage from St. Cyril of Jerusalem in a letter dated January 1, 1956. Thereafter, she returns to the passage again and again because, as her commentary suggests, St. Cyril provides her with a concrete image embodying the truth that lies at the foundation of her fiction: that every good story is about the inevitable confrontation between the individual human person and the force that is most likely to undermine her, body and soul.

The dragon takes many forms in O'Connor's stories as each of her protagonists meets a nemesis that challenges everything he or she believes. The character's response to that shocking and often violent encounter with the enemy determines whether he or she will be destroyed or will be able to continue along the road to salvation. We see this fateful encounter in the clash between the grandmother and the Misfit and in the struggle between Hulga and Manley Pointer (as well as among other characters)—battles wherein the protagonist emerges chastened, yet profoundly altered. Clearly, the outcome of each story is important, but the heart of the drama lies in the dynamics of the struggle.

This is true of O'Connor's story, as well. As she was writing about the dragons her characters were facing, she was facing her own, primarily in the form of the disease that was gradually robbing her of her strength, her energy, and her ability to practice her art. From 1959–63, after the brief period of improvement she experienced following her pilgrimage to Lourdes, O'Connor suffered a series of setbacks in her health. She developed necrosis of the jaw, making eating difficult and requiring her to take large doses of aspirin to dull the pain. This new development, as well as the ongoing disintegration of her hipbones, forced her physicians to lower the doses of her steroid drugs; she would then need injections of Novocain and cortisone directly into her hips to offer her at least temporary cessation from the pain. The various operations available at the time—including hip replacement and bone grafts—were ruled out for fear that surgery would aggravate her lupus.

Despite all of these crippling physical ailments, O'Connor continued to publish her work, to win literary prizes, including first prize in the O. Henry Awards for "Everything That Rises Must Converge," and to travel to colleges and universities across the country to lecture and to read her stories, occasioning trips to Texas, Louisiana, Missouri, Minnesota, Virginia, Maryland, Massachusetts, and Washington DC, among other places. At these events, O'Connor was treated with great respect—even at her relatively young age—and like the famous writer she had become. She was enjoying what few writers do—recognition of the value of her work during her own lifetime.

Yet, O'Connor was not content. Though she was feted, the recipient of awards and honorary doctorates, she was unhappy in her writing, troubled by the fact that she was producing few stories and that she was not at work on a new novel. Her energy was flagging, so much so that she wrote to a friend, "I appreciate and need your prayers. I've been writing eighteen years and I've reached the point where I can't do again what I know I can do well, and the larger things that I need to do now, I doubt my capacity for doing."[2] Finally, and unexpectedly, Flannery had a breakthrough. Exhausted by fatigue, diagnosed as anemia, O'Connor was forced to spend many of her afternoon hours in the waiting room of the doctor's office in Milledgeville where she received iron treatments. O'Connor had always received inspiration for her stories from the people she lived among, and, now, surrounded by country women and their ailing husbands, observing their mystery and their manners, listening to Southern small talk for hours at a time, she was once again moved to make art of their lives, creating one of her finest stories, "Revelation." In eight weeks, between public speaking appearances, she produced a draft of the story, announcing to her friend Maryat Lee, "I have writ a story for which I am, for the time anyway, pleased, pleased, pleased."[3]

"Revelation"

Ruby Turpin, the main protagonist in "Revelation," is one of O'Connor's larger-than-life women, in every sense of the term. Physically large and imposing, she takes up a lot of room in the tiny doctor's office, where the reader first meets her, along with her husband Claud, but she also takes up a lot of psychic space. Mrs. Turpin fancies herself a connoisseur of humanity, casting her eye about the place, sizing up her fellow human beings, and judging their worth based on their cleanliness, appearance, speech, and, most notably, their shoes. Possessed of a kind of rage for social order, Mrs. Turpin would go to sleep at night, categorizing people according to a rigid hierarchy in terms of race and class:

> On the bottom of the heap were most colored people. . . . then next to them—not above, just away from—were the white-trash; then above them were the home-owners, and about them the home-and-land owners, to which she and Claud belonged. Above she and Claud were people with a lot of money and much bigger houses and much more land. But here the complexity of it would begin to bear in on her, for some of the people with a lot of money were common and ought to be below she and Claud and some of the people who had good blood had lost their money and had to rent and then there were colored people who owned their homes and land as well. . . . Usually by the time she had fallen asleep all the classes of people were moiling and roiling around in her head, and she would dream they were all crammed in together in a box car, being ridden off to be put in a gas oven.[4]

Mrs. Turpin is both a racist and a bigot—identities she is unaware of—and owing to this lack of self-knowledge, she also believes she is "saved," in the Southern Protestant lingo of her place and era. She does not recognize the darkness of her own dreams, the image of the boxcars and gas ovens echoing the Holocaust, embodiment of another culture with a rage for social order, one that turned murderous. Instead, she congratulates herself on her piety, publicly professing her love of Jesus, singing along to the gospel songs on the radio, and thanking God for having been so good to her. She sees no contradiction between her contempt for other human beings and her identity as a Christian: "If it's one thing I am . . . it's grateful. When I think who all I could have been besides myself and what all I got, a little of everything, and a good disposition besides, I just feel like shouting, 'Thank you, Jesus, for making everything the way it is!' . . . 'Oh thank you, Jesus, Jesus, thank you!' "[5]

Mrs. Turpin bears all the marks of an O'Connor character who is sorely in need of a wake-up call. Unaware of her spiritual peril, too blinded by her own (supposed) virtues to see her sins, it will take some sort of shocking, violent event to dislodge her from her complacent state and force her to see herself as she truly is. That event comes, reliably and in the nick of time, in the form of a book entitled *Human Development*, hurled across the room by a homely young woman named Mary Grace, Ruby Turpin's nemesis. Ruby has seen the girl reading her book and glancing up often to eye her with fierce contempt, but could not possibly understand why the young woman might have conceived such a virulent hatred for her. After the girl has struck her with the book, just above her left eye, Mrs. Turpin's vision is immediately altered. At first, the room and all the people in it seem small and distant, and then her vision reverses itself so everything appears larger than it is. The world no longer seems as certain as it did before. Instinctively, Mrs. Turpin feels as if the girl knows her in some essential way and has a message to deliver: "What you got to say to me?" she asks and waits, holding her breath "as for a revelation." The girl's response to this woman of supposed virtue is stunning: "Go back to hell where you came from, you old wart hog."[6]

Mrs. Turpin may be a racist and a bigot, but she (like any other sinner) is not beyond hope. The aptly named Mary Grace has delivered a disturbing but potentially salvific annunciation to Ruby, and she is haunted by it for the remainder of the story. She cannot rest without seeing the image of the hog, an unredeemed and biblically unclean creature, as a version of herself, casting her in a new light wherein all of her ugliness is suddenly evident. In her confusion and rage, Ruby tries to share the message with Claud, but she cannot bear to have her beloved husband think of her this way; she tries to share it with the black field hands who work on her farm, but they refuse to take Mrs. Turpin's distress seriously and treat her with condescension. In the end, she takes her case directly to God. Walking across the fields toward the hogs, creatures she must wash and feed and keep alive, "She had the look of a woman going single-handed, weaponless, into battle."[7] In the light of the setting sun (wherein, once again, O'Connor invokes the identity between the sun and the Son), she asks God a question and demands an answer, "How am I a hog and me both?" Ruby's view, until now, has been too schematic, as her faulty class system would suggest, too black and white. One is either good or evil, saved or damned, a sinner or a saint—such theology makes no allowances for human complexity, the role of saving grace, and the mercy of God. Her soliloquy culminates in a final surge of fury that shakes her as she roars, "Who do you think you are?" [8]

The answer Ruby receives is twofold. First, she is given a glimpse of the mystery of the world she inhabits, one that is suffused with divine presence. Even the pigs in the pen before her "pant with a secret life." Mrs. Turpin, large as she is, realizes how small and vulnerable the individual human person is, how dependent upon God all creatures are. And then, in one final, fantastic, visionary moment, she sees the heavenly procession of the communion of saints:

> She saw the streak [in the sky] as a vast swinging bridge extending upward from the earth through a field of living fire. Upon it a vast horde of souls were rumbling toward heaven. There were whole companies of white-trash, clean for the first time in their lives, and bands of black niggers in white robes, and battalions of freaks and lunatics shouting and clapping and leaping like frogs. And bringing up the end of the procession was a tribe of people whom she recognized at once as those who, like herself and Claud, had always had a little of everything and the God-given wit to use it right. She leaned forward to observe them closer. They were marching behind the others with great dignity, accountable as they had always been for good order and common sense and respectable behavior. They alone were on key. Yet she could see by their shocked and altered faces that even their virtues were being burned away."[9]

Ruby's vision is a clear corrective to the coarse classification system she had lived by, to her bigoted view of blacks and poor whites, the disabled, the insane, and all other human beings she thought were beneath her. To the contrary, the heavenly procession is a concrete embodiment of the biblical maxim, "The Last Shall Be First." While these—the sinned-against, the marginalized, and the dispossessed—are much beloved of God and received first into the kingdom, the self-righteous and supposedly virtuous bring up the rear. The good news is there is a place for them in the kingdom; the bad news, for Ruby, is that the place is not nearly as august as she had imagined.

At the end of the story, Mrs. Turpin is utterly altered. The message of Mary Grace and the vision she conjures enables her to see her sinful nature and her true place in the schema of salvation. What's more, this knowledge arrives in sufficient time to enable her to amend her ways, to at least attempt give up her hasty judgments and petty hatreds, and to live a good life. Grace has been extended to her, though the reader cannot know whether she will accept it. Ruby Turpin meets her dragon on her way to the father of souls, and, in this particular encounter, she is not devoured.

Last Acts

O'Connor's recovery of her creative powers reinvigorated her imagination, but, unfortunately, her body would not cooperate with the new surge of life she felt in her mind and heart. Shortly after completing "Revelation," just before Christmas of 1963, Flannery fainted and had to spend more than a week in bed. A physical exam showed evidence of a fibroid tumor—likely the cause of her anemia—and the need for a hysterectomy. Despite the danger of reactivating her lupus, the surgery was performed, and by March 25, her thirty-ninth birthday, the disease had returned. Perhaps sensing the fact that she did not have much time left, Flannery worked diligently from her sick bed for the next several months, trying to complete two unfinished stories, "Judgement Day" and "Parker's Back," for inclusion in what would be her final collection of short stories, *Everything That Rises Must Converge*. She continued this work, as she went in and out of the hospital, undergoing blood transfusions to keep up her strength, the doctors treating her for repeated infections and high blood pressure. When away from her typewriter, she hid her manuscripts beneath her pillow, for fear she would be forbidden to work, writing out her stories in long hand when the nurses and visitors were absent.

She took particular delight in "Parker's Back," the story of a young man who once believed himself to be "ordinary as a loaf of bread" but falls in love with tattoos, an art that could transform the body into a vision of beauty, wholeness, and perfection. His pursuit of the perfectly tattooed body is foolish and futile, a quixotic quest, but it is an embodiment of his hunger for the holy, his desire to see the divine incarnated in everyday people and in everyday life. She had begun the story three years earlier and was pleased to be able to complete it.

As O'Connor grew weaker, she continued her correspondence as best she could. Her letters grew shorter. "Prayers requested," she wrote to her friend Louise Abbot, "I am sick of being sick."[10] It was during these last days that she laboriously copied out the Prayer of St. Raphael, the prayer she said every day, to send to her friend Janet McKane, who was also ailing, reminding them both that their true home and destination was "the province of joy." No longer able to attend Mass and receive the Eucharist, on July 7, she requested and received the sacrament of Anointing of the Sick from the Sacred Heart parish priest.

She would not live to see her last book of stories published—it would come out the following year—but she was gratified at the news that the story with which she had been "pleased, pleased, pleased," just a few months before,

"Revelation," won first prize in the O. Henry Awards. It must have been some small source of solace to know that she had created art that would outlive her, that would continue to do good in the world long after she was unable to. In a sense, she was not needed any more—her work had taken on a life of its own. On July 29, O'Connor was taken by ambulance to the hospital for the last time. She slipped into a coma on August 2 and died of kidney failure shortly after midnight on August 3.

Until her very last hours, Flannery's mind was on her life's work. For thirteen long years, she lived with her lupus daily, an affliction, a cross, a companion, a terrible fiend and friend. She never despaired, never felt sorry for herself, never used her illness as an excuse for not practicing her difficult and demanding vocation. Like the strong women protagonists she had created, Flannery had faced and fought the dragon. And she had won.

A funeral Mass was held for Mary Flannery O'Connor on August 4 at 11:00 a.m. at Sacred Heart Church. It was attended by a sizeable number of people, all of them locals. There wasn't sufficient time for her many friends, those in New York and other far-flung places, to make the journey to Milledgeville. She was buried that same day beside her father in the Memory Hill Cemetery. Her earthly pilgrimage ended, she had, indeed, come home to stay.

The Legacy

In *The Letter of His Holiness John Paul II to Artists, 1999,* the pope describes the artist's essential role in creating and maintaining the complex nexus between art and faith: "True art has a close affinity with the world of faith, so that, even in situations where culture and the Church are far apart,

art remains a kind of bridge to religious experience. In so far as it seeks the beautiful, fruit of an imagination which rises above the everyday, art is by its nature a kind of appeal to the mystery. Even when they explore the darkest depths of the soul or the most unsettling aspects of evil, artists give voice . . . to the universal desire for redemption."[11]

An artist and a poet himself, John Paul II knew from experience the artist's compulsion to engage mystery, to explore the unseen by means of the seen, and to cultivate a voice and vision with sufficient range to express the whole scale of human suffering yet, at the same time, hold out hope for deliverance from the evils that afflict us. In living out this vocation, the writer embarks on a journey as both artist and human being that will inevitably take him or her to dark places, a Calvary path that informs the work and the life.

Flannery O'Connor walked that path. She looked into the darkness of the human heart, and out of that darkness she created stories of great resonance and power. O'Connor's stories speak their own idiom: her voice is like no one else's, incorporating language that is both lofty and local, biblical in its urgency and human in its poignancy, and encompassing both the comedy and tragedy of human existence. Her stories capture the daily-ness of her time and place, and transcend particular human circumstance to address the universality of human experience. Her subject is the mystery of the human personality, operative in all times and all places, and her stories reveal her deep respect for that mystery and the holiness it harbors. O'Connor's art is an act of faith—a means through which she glimpsed the human, the divine, and the invisible nexus that connects the two—and then she passed those glimpses on to her readers. The gifts Flannery left us are many—thirty-two short stories, two novels, a dozen (plus) essays, and hundreds of letters—but the greatest gift, perhaps, is that of her life. Blessed with brilliance, fired by faith, yet physically fragile, flawed and fraught, Flannery lived and died with grace and wit and sheer nerve. Not bad for a life lived between the house and the chicken yard.

Notes

Introduction—pages 1–9

1. Ralph C. Wood, "Such a Catholic," *National Review* (March 9, 2009): 38.

2. FOC to Betty Hester, April 4, 1958, *HB*, 275.

3. FOC to Betty Hester, June 28, 1956, *HB*, 163.

Chapter One—pages 11–30

1. FOC to Betty Hester, July 5, 1958, *HB*, 290–91.

2. FOC to Janet McKane, May 17, 1963, *HB*, 520.

3. Brad Gooch, *Flannery: A Life of Flannery O'Connor* (New York: Little, Brown, 2009), 16–17.

4. Garry Wills, *Bare Ruined Choirs: Doubt, Prophecy, and Radical Religion* (New York: Doubleday, 1972), 15, 37.

5. *MM*, 3.

6. FOC to Betty Hester, January 17, 1956, *HB*, 131–32.

7. FOC to Ben Griffith, March 3, 1954, *CW*, 923.

8. *CS*, 238.

9. Ibid., 243.

10. Ibid., 246.

11. Ibid., 247.

12. Ibid., 248.

13. Gooch, *Flannery*, 27.

14. FOC to Betty Hester, July 28, 1956, *HB*, 168.

15. Sally Fitzgerald, "Rooms with a View," *Flannery O'Connor Bulletin* 10 (1981): 17.

16. Gooch, *Flannery*, 52.

17. FOC to Ben Griffith, February 13, 1954, *HB*, 68–69.

18. Gooch, *Flannery*, 53.

19. Sally Fitzgerald, "A Master Class: From the Correspondence of Caroline Gordon and Flannery O'Connor," *Georgia Review*, vol. 33, no. 4, 831.

20. Gooch, *Flannery*, 76.

21. FOC to Betty Hester, August 28, 1955, *HB*, 98.

22. Ibid.

23. Gooch, *Flannery*, 80.

24. Ibid., 90.

25. Paul Elie, *The Life You Save May Be Your Own: An American Pilgrimage* (New York: Farrar, Straus and Giroux, 2003), 135.

Chapter Two—pages 31–42

1. Flannery O'Connor, *A Prayer Journal* (New York: Farrar, Straus and Giroux, 2013), 5.

2. Jonathan Rogers, *The Terrible Speed of Mercy* (Nashville: Thomas Nelson, 2012), 24.

3. Elie, *The Life*, 146.

4. FOC to Roslyn Barnes, December 12, 1960, *HB*, 422.

5. W. A. Sessions, "Introduction," in *A Prayer Journal* (New York: Farrar, Straus and Giroux, 2013), viii.

6. O'Connor, *A Prayer Journal*, 10–11.

7. Ibid., 38.

8. Ibid., 39.

9. FOC to Betty Hester, August 28, 1955, *HB*, 98–99.

10. Elie, *The Life*, 149.

11. *MM*, 103.

12. Ibid., 98.

13. Ibid., 176.

14. Ibid., 167.

15. Ibid., 112.

16. Ibid., 34.

17. Gooch, *Flannery*, 127.

18. *CW*, 1241.

Chapter Three—pages 43–61

1. FOC to Elizabeth Ames, July 27, 1948, O'Connor Guest File, Yaddo.

2. FOC to Maryat Lee, February 24, 1957, *HB*, 204.

3. *CW*, 1242.

4. FOC, *Wise Blood,* Preface to Second Edition, (New York: Farrar, Straus and Giroux, 1962).

5. *MM*, 171.

6. Ibid., 185.

7. Gooch, *Flannery*, 160.

8. FOC to Betty Hester, April 21, 1956, *HB*, 152.

9. Elie, *The Life*, 172.

10. Ibid.

11. Gooch, *Flannery*, 172.

12. *CW*, 1096.

13. FOC to Betty Hester, June 1, 1956, *HB*, 161.

14. Gooch, *Flannery*, 177.

15. FOC to Janet McKane, June 5, 1963, *HB*, 523.

16. FOC to Betty Hester, December 16, 1955, *HB* 124–25.

17. Ibid.

18. *CS*, 119.

19. Ian Hamilton, *Robert Lowell: A Biography* (New York: Vintage, 1983), 149–50.

20. FOC to Betty Hester, April 21, 1956, *HB,* 152.

21. FOC to Robie Macauley, *CW,* 886.

22. *Flannery O'Connor Bulletin* 6, 1977: 79.

23. FOC to Mavis McIntosh, October 31, 1949, *HB,* 17.

24. Robert Fitzgerald, introduction, *Everything That Rises Must Converge* (New York: Macmillan, 1965), xvi.

25. *HB*, 22.

Chapter Four—pages 62–74

1. FOC to Betty Hester, June 28, 1956, *HB,* 163.

2. Gooch, *Flannery*, 215.

3. FOC to Betty Hester, November 25, 1955, *HB*, 117–18.

4. Elie, *The Life*, 193.

5. Ibid., 192.

6. *MM*, 14–15.

7. Ibid., 10.

8. FOC to Betty Hester, November 25, 1955, *HB*, 118.

9. *CS*, 194.

10. Ibid., 226.

11. Elie, *The Life*, 496.

12. Fitzgerald, "A Master Class," 831.

13. Elie, *The Life*, 199, 501.

14. Gooch, *Flannery*, 208.

15. FOC to Robie Macauley, May 18, 1955, *HB*, 81.

16. *MM*, 185.

17. Fitzgerald, "A Master Class," 831.

18. Gooch, *Flannery*, 201.

19. *CW*, 1037.

Chapter Five—pages 75–88

1. FOC to Betty Hester, July 20, 1955, *HB*, 90.

2. *CW*, 1245.

3. *CS*, 150.

4. Ibid., 146.

5. O'Connor, *Wise Blood*, 109.

6. *CS*, 152.

7. Ibid., 154.

8. Ibid., 155.

9. Gooch, *Flannery*, 222–23.

10. Ibid., 228.

11. FOC to Betty Hester, June 28, 1956, *HB,* 163–64.

12. *CS*, 272–73.

13. Ibid., 276.

14. Ibid.

15. Ibid., 275.

16. Quoted in *Flannery*, Gooch, 258; March 1, 1955, GSCU.

17. Elie, *The Life*, 233.

18. Gooch, *Flannery*, 233.

19. Ibid., 252.

20. Ibid., 256

21. Ibid., 257.

Chapter Six—pages 89–98

1. FOC to Betty Hester, January 17, 1956, *HB*, 132.

2. FOC to Betty Hester, April 7, 1956, *HB*, 151.

3. George Herbert, *The Complete English Poems* (New York: Penguin, 2005), 57.

4. Emily Dickinson, *The Complete Poems of Emily Dickinson*, edited by Thomas H. Johnson (New York: Little, Brown, 1957), 123.

5. Angela Alaimo O'Donnell, *The Province of Joy: Praying with Flannery O'Connor* (Brewster, MA: Paraclete Press, 2012), 15–16.

6. FOC to Janet McKane, July 14, 1964, *HB*, 592–93.

7. Elie, *The Life*, 264.

8. FOC to Robie Macauley, May 18, 1955, *HB*, 82.

9. FOC to Betty Hester, July 20, 1955, *HB*, 90.

10. Jonathan Rogers, *The Terrible Speed of Mercy* (Nashville: Thomas Nelson, 2012), 102–3.

11. FOC to Betty Hester, July 20, 1955, *HB*, 90.

12. FOC to Betty Hester, August 2, 1955, *HB*, 92.

13. FOC to Betty Hester, January 17, 1956, *HB*, 130.

14. Elie, *The Life*, 271.

15. FOC to Betty Hester, March 24, 1956, *HB*, 150.

16. Elie, *The Life*, 267.

17. Ibid., 285–86.

18. FOC to Betty Hester, November 2, 1957, *HB*, 250, and FOC to Elizabeth Bishop, June 1, 1958, *HB*, 286.

19. *CW*, 1251.

20. FOC to Sally and Robert Fitzgerald, May 11, 1958, *CW*, 1069.

Chapter Seven—pages 99–112

1. FOC to Louise Abbot, undated 1959, *HB*, 354.

2. FOC to Betty Hester, October 3, 1959, *HB*, 351.

3. FOC to Sally and Robert Fitzgerald, mid-September, 1951, *HB*, 27.

4. FOC to John Hawkes, September 13, 1959, *HB*, 349.

5. Ibid., 350.

6. *Time,* February 1960, 118–19.

7. Flannery O'Connor, *The Violent Bear It Away* (New York: Farrar, Straus and Giroux, 1955), 21.

8. *MM*, 112.

9. FOC to Betty Hester, October 1, 1960, *HB*, 411.

10. Flannery O'Connor, "In the Devil's Territory," in *Flannery O'Connor: Spiritual Writings* (Maryknoll, NY: Orbis, 2003), 128–29.

11. O'Connor, *The Violent,* 240.

12. Ibid., 239.

13. Elie, *The Life*, 327.

14. Robie Macauley, *Esprit: Journal of Thought and Opinion,* 8, no. 1 (Scranton, PA: University of Scranton, Winter 1964): 34, quoted in Gooch, *Flannery*, 125.

15. FOC to Maryat Lee, April 25, 1959, *HB*, 329.

16. FOC to Maryat Lee, January 9, 1957, *HB*, 195.

17. Gooch, *Flannery*, 335.

18. FOC to Betty Hester, August 2, 1955, *HB*, 92.

19. FOC to Roslyn Barnes, March 29, 1961, *HB*, 438.

20. *CS*, 420.

21. Flannery O'Connor, *The Violent*, 20.

Chapter Eight—pages 113–24

1. *MM*, 35.

2. FOC to Sister Mariella Gable, May 4, 1963, *HB*, 518.

3. FOC to Maryat Lee, November 29, 1963, *HB*, 551.

4. *CS*, 491–92.

5. Ibid., 499.

6. Ibid., 500.

7. Ibid., 505.

8. Ibid., 506–07.

9. Ibid., 508.

10. FOC to Louise Abbot, May 28, 1964, *CW*, 1210.

11. Pope John Paul II, Letter to Artists, April 4, 1999, http://www
.vatican.va/holy_father/john_paul_ii/letters/documents/hf_jp-ii
_let_23041999_artists_en.html.

Index

Abbot, Louise: letter to, 99, 121
Accent (journal), 41
ACTH (the corticosteroid), 63, 65, 76, 114; results of, 86
America (Jesuit weekly magazine), 96
American Association of University Women, 97
Andalusia (farm), 12, 66–67, 69, 75, 80, 98. *See also* Georgia; Milledgeville
Anointing of the Sick, 121
art: and faith, 8, 32, 39, 47, 90, 96, 122–23; Metropolitan Museum of, 54
arthritis. *See* lupus: false diagnosis of arthritis
As I Lay Dying (Faulkner), 59
Atlanta, 23–24, 64, 95
Augustine, Saint, 94

Baldwin General Hospital, 61
Baldwin, James, 105–6
baptism, 65, 101
Barnes, Roslyn, 110
Beiswanger, Dr. George, 29

birds. *See* chickens; peacocks
birth, of O'Connor, 13
Bulletin, The (the Atlanta diocesan weekly), 96

cartoons, 26–29
Catherine of Siena, Saint, 94
Catholicism: in America, 15, 71; and being different, 15–16, 24, 46, 93; and children, 20; in context of mainstream literary establishment, 55–56; and conversion, 48–49, 52–53, 57, 94; culture of, 18, 37; and education, 16–19, 25, 27, 28, 33; in exile, 5, 13; influence on work, 6–9; Irish, 14–16, 18; and literature, 9, 48, 59; prejudice/suspicion toward, 1–2, 15; in Protestant culture, 15, 23–24, 49; and the South, 4–5, 14; theology of, 8, 18, 39, 48, 63, 72, 77, 90, 96, 109–10. *See also* church; faith; writer: Catholic